Green Thumb
Wisdom

Green Thumb Wisdom

Doc and Katy Abraham

Illustrated by
Darryl Abraham

A Storey Publishing Book

Storey Communications, Inc.
Schoolhouse Road
Pownal, Vermont 05261

*The mission of Storey Communications is to serve our customers
by publishing practical information that encourages personal independence
in harmony with the environment.*

Edited by Elizabeth McHale
Cover design by Meredith Maker
Text design and production by Cynthia McFarland
Production assistance by Susan Bernier
Indexed by Northwind Editorial Services

Printed in the United States by R.R. Donnelley
10 9 8 7 6 5 4 3 2 1

Library of Congress Cataloging-in-Publication Data

Abraham, George, [date]
    Green Thumb Wisdom / Doc and Katy Abraham.
        p.   cm.
    "A Storey Publishing book."
    ISBN 0-88266-928-1
    1. Gardening.   2. Gardening—United States.   I. Abraham, Katy.
II. Title.
    SB453.A256   1996
    635—dc20   95-46682
                                                            CIP

CONTENTS

Introduction

If you beat your nut tree with a baseball bat, you can force it to bear nuts. *Wrong!* You risk injuring your tree.

Dumping a bucket of nails around your hydrangea bush encourages it to blossom. *Not a chance!* You'll only end up with a nice collection of rusty nails.

You should water African violets and other plants from the bottom only. *False!* You can water your houseplants from the top or the bottom. It makes no difference to a thirsty plant! (However, African violets *do not* like cold water on their leaves.)

Webster defines a myth as a falsehood; an unfounded belief. These three bits of gardening folklore are among the myths debunked in this book.

In our 48 years of garden writing (that's 96 years combined), we've collected garden lore from the world over. Gardeners who read our columns and listen to our television and radio shows and attend our workshops have sent us garden myths for "testing" in our greenhouse and nursery operations. We conducted our research with the help of other experienced gardeners and horticultural experts.

1

We decided to write this book to separate fact from fiction in gardening lore. Some of these myths are harmless and do little more than waste a gardener's valuable time. Others could harm you or your plants, or cost you money. Our goal is to shed some light on those beliefs that are erroneous and to enable gardeners to get even more enjoyment and productivity from the nation's most popular hobby.

Any book of this nature is a collaboration, and thanks are due to many. Some of the best "gardening brains" in the country helped to search and research, test and retest the material you will find in the pages that follow. Michael Warren Thomas, America's Naturally Green Expert, provided invaluable help. Help was also given by the editorial staffs of many of America's fine magazines, including *Organic Gardening, Horticulture, National Gardening, Fine Gardening, Flower and Garden, House Plant, Hobby Greenhouse, Harrowsmith Country Life,* and *Nursery Business.* The staffs offered opinions and advice and have done a good job of keeping gardening myths from propagating. We want to express our gratitude to our good friend Chet Walker, co-host of our weekly radio

program. For years he has encouraged listeners to send us their questions and comments through radio station WHAM in Rochester, New York.

Special appreciation goes to our good friends Bob and Mary Jane Mann, who help us sort the thousands of letters that arrive each week in the Green Thumb mail and who helped select the myths included in this book. Thanks also go to Deborah Allison, whose wordprocessing expertise made life more bearable in the Abraham household while the book went from first to final draft. Our gratitude goes to Gwen Steege, our editor, whose confidence, encouragement, and faith were unflagging. Also thanks to Elizabeth McHale for her keen editorial touch and to talented designers Meredith Maker and Cindy McFarland.

As with our previous books, this too was a family affair. Our thanks to our son Darryl and our daughter Leanna and their families for their interest and support throughout. And we would be remiss if we didn't acknowledge the contribution made by our Labrador retrievers, Mirabelle and Razzi, whose ravenous appetites ensured that we got up early every morning to have plenty of time to research and write.

And very special thanks to the hundreds of thousands of "Green Thumb" friends in the Rochester area of New York and around the nation. You have long been the source of our inspiration and inquiry — sharing your tips and sending us your tough gardening problems.

Other books by Doc and Katy Abraham

Green Thumb Garden Handbook
Green Thumb Book of Fruits and Vegetables
Green Thumb Book of Indoor Gardening
Green Thumb Tricks for the Classroom
How to Grow Vegetables without a Garden
Organic Gardening under Glass
Houseplant Rx
The New Green Thumb Garden Handbook
How to Grow Plants from Seed
Green Thumb Book of Houseplants

In addition to the titles above, Doc and Katy Abraham collaborated to write the *U.S. Department of Agriculture Yearbook 1977* and helped write *10,000 Garden Questions Answered.*

1. Houseplants

Certain indoor plants are odor eaters and helpful in clearing the air in a room.

Plants advertised as "odor eaters" or "odor controllers" don't exist. The ads guarantee these plants to leave your bathroom, kitchen, or entire home smelling like a gardenia. Some go so far as to say they kill odors from pets, garbage, mold, onions, garlic, and cigarette smoke.

There are scented plants (e.g., scented geraniums) that give an aroma of cinnamon, lemon, pineapple, or lime. These contain a natural deodorizer, but they don't squirt the smell into the air. Most of these only emit fragrance when the leaves come into contact with something else. For example, only when you brush up against a scented geranium does it emit any fragrance.

Several readers tell us that a raw potato makes a cheap and effective refrigerator deodorizer. Or try a bouquet of eucalyptus sprigs in the home to help.

It is important to water African violets and other potted plants from the bottom only.

We used to believe that it was best to water from the top for a period, then switch to bottom watering. Anne Tinari, one of the country's leading growers, says that this is wrong. Water from the top *or* the bottom. If you water from the top, avoid getting a lot of water on the leaves of African violets, to avoid causing permanent spots.

Many houseplants love having their leaves washed, but cold water can cause ugly yellow spots on African violet leaves unless they are allowed to dry out of direct sunlight.

Violet fanciers have great luck using wickwatering. It's simple: Insert a short piece of nylon yarn though the soil in the pot and pull one end through the drainage hole. Then, set the pot on top of a plastic tub in which you have cut a small hole in the lid. Fill the tub with water and some liquid plant food, put the lid on, and let the string drop through the hole and into the solution. Set the pot on top of the lid. Refill the "tub" as needed. This way, the plant will be able to take up water and nutrients as needed.

My neighbor raises good African violets using boiled water from potatoes. Isn't that a good way to introduce fungus problems?

No. Since I married a potato farmer's daughter, I have to sing the praises of that wonderful vegetable, the potato. It's the biggest food bargain we have today. When cooking spuds, leave the skins on, as the portion just under the skin contains twice the solids of the rest. Peeling removes 20 to 25 percent of the total weight. If peeled and boiled in water, 20 percent of the solid nutrients are lost, whereas most of the nutrients are conserved if spuds are unpeeled.

The water from boiled potatoes is loaded with nutrients such as nitrogen, phosphorous, and potassium, plus other minor elements that are beneficial to plants as well as humans. And since the water is boiled, no fungus could survive.

The books say you should not set potted plants in a saucer of water.

There's no reason why you cannot place shallow saucers under your plants. In fact, it's a good idea because this "forbidden" technique results in savings of water and plant nutrients. The water that normally is lost through the bottom of the pot is caught in the saucer, giving plants more time to absorb it. Empty any water that remains after 24 hours. Saucered plants need less water and less plant food. One nurseryman studied the effects of shallow plastic saucers under his potted mums in a greenhouse and found that the saucered plants needed only 8 ounces (280 ml) of water per plant, compared to as much as 32 ounces (1.1 liters) for plants without the saucers. The amount of soluble fertilizer applied was reduced by ½ to ¾ because it too was caught. You shouldn't put potted plants in deep saucers of water, as it will shut off oxygen to the roots. Shallow saucers work fine and can prevent water from ruining your table top.

If you water your houseplants and the water comes right out of the bottom holes of the pot, that means they don't need watering.

You should water a plant until water seeps out of the holes in the bottom of the pot. But in this case, the soil was so dry it couldn't absorb any water and the water *rushed right out,* only teasing the plants. When a soil ball dries out, it shrinks away from inside the pot's wall, leaving a space for water to leak out. Hanging baskets dry out quickly and need to be watered more often. Feel the soil. For most plants, the soil should be slightly moist at all times. Another test is to lift the pot to check its weight. Light means dry. When a soil is bone-dry, you can't water from the top. Place the pot in a pan of water and let it soak from bottom up for 30 minutes. If the leaves are wilted, this is a good time for a warm shower — except for African violets.

My wife thinks I need a therapist. I often take a shower with my houseplants.

Tell your wife you don't need a therapist. A lot of people take a shower with their plants. A gentle warm shower is one of the biggest treats for most plants, especially hard-leaved tropicals such as rubber plants and philodendrons. Even hairy-leaved plants such as African violets don't mind a misting or a shower as long as the water is warm and the drops don't remain on the leaves for very long. Do it in the morning so the leaves can dry off in the sunny part of the day, but not in direct sunlight. If the leaves are wet at night they could rot or mildew.

Most houseplants should be allowed to go dry before you water again.

The toughest question we get is how often to water houseplants. Books are full of conflicting advice about this. Some say to let plants go dry between waterings, some say to keep the plants soaked, and some say to let plants go on the dry side always. Most houseplants need soil that is kept slightly moist, never soggy, and never very dry. Uniform moisture is more beneficial than swings from very wet to very dry — which tend to be the most damaging to the roots and can damage the leaves. Most plants are able to tolerate the lower humidity indoors, provided they have adequate moisture at the roots and adequate roots to absorb the moisture. When both are low, leaf damage is more common and more severe. It shows up as tip burn, scorched edges, or entire leaves turning brown.

A safe rule is to keep the soil uniformly moistened, which means watering when the soil starts to dry, about two or three times a week, especially in winter when humidity levels are low and drying heat is on. Do not water if soil feels moist or soggy to the touch. According to Yoder Brothers, North America's largest propagator of chrysanthemums, over 53 percent of customers let potted mums wilt for lack of water. Every time a plant wilts, it will lose between one and four days of flowering life, the company says.

Some plants tolerate dryness more than others. When you purchase a plant, always get growing instructions. Then follow those instructions and observe how well the plant does.

It's impossible to grow healthy plants indoors because they get leggy from too much heat, lack of light, overfeeding, and so on.

False. As plants grow upward they often lose their lower leaves. The tops of the plants may be attractive, but the bare stems can be an eyesore. Some plants, such as Norfolk Island pine, grow up to 250 feet tall in their native environment, so you can see why they may grow out-of-bounds indoors. High temperatures and low light induce legginess as well, as does excess fertilizer. Soil that is kept too dry, on the other hand, limits plant growth.

After an overcast winter and as days become longer, the light is brighter, making houseplants start growing with renewed vigor. It is at this time of year that you should consider severely pruning them to reduce their height. Some plants that grow tall and tolerate severe pruning include the dumbcane *(Dieffenbachia)*, several corn plants *(Dracena)*, rubber plant and weeping fig *(Ficus sp.)*, umbrella tree *(Schefflera)*, and spider aralia *(Dizygotheca)*. Add the

geranium *(Pelargonium)* and poinsettia *(Euphorbia pulcherrima)* to the list.

Plants that get too tall need not be discarded; they can be pruned to reduce their height. When you prune many plants, you stimulate them to send out side shoots that make them bushy on the lower trunk. Save the tops and root them in moist perlite or vermiculite.

What can be done to compensate for shortage of light in the winter?

Winter light is half that of summer for several reasons: There are more cloudy days, daylight hours are fewer, and the sun is lower in the sky. There are several things you can do at home to increase the light your plants are receiving:

✔Prune or thin any outdoor plants that shade the windows. This will let more light into the house.

✔ Increase the reflected light (paint interior walls white).

✔ Stand plants on trays of white marble chips or perlite, or use mirrors, to increase the amount of reflected light.

✔Rinse dust and grime off leaves, using warm or soapy water. This not only allows more light to strike the leaves, it also discourages spider mites and other pests.

To grow good houseplants, you really need a light meter.

You can measure light with a light meter, or you can use what is called the "hand-shadow" test. To use the hand-shadow test, hold your hand about 8 to 12 inches above the plant or spot where you want a plant to grow. There are three classes of natural light intensities your hand will identify:

✔Direct or high light. A southern window usually gives you high light.

✔ **Medium light.** You get a fuzzy but definite shadow if you hold your hand over a spot. You get this in a sunny window with an eastern or western exposure. Most foliage plants need this type of light, including asparagus fern, grape ivy, *Dieffenbachia, Dracena,* philodendron, Swedish ivy, snake plant, and wandering Jew.

✔ **Low light intensity.** You get only an indistinct or faint shadow when you hold your hand over a spot on the plant. A shaded window or northern exposure gives you low light intensity. Actually, most homes have low light, but some plants that will grow well in low light include maiden-hair fern, cast iron plant, waffle plant, holly fern, and bella palm.

If you have enough light to read by, you have enough light to grow plants satisfactorily.

Enough light to read by is one thing, but enough to grow plants is something else. A few plants tolerant of low light may survive, but many will not thrive. In case you're wondering about the terms "low light" or "foot candles," we'll explain: Low light refers to 50 to 500 foot candles; medium light, 500 to 3,000 foot candles; and high light, 3,000 to 8,000 foot candles.

Plants grow lopsided because the soil lacks certain nutrients.

No. When a plant grows lopsided, it is usually because of light. If you want symmetrical growth, give your plants a quarter turn each time you water — or at least on a regular basis, such as every week or so.

Some people think this disturbs a plant's north-south alignment, affecting their ability to absorb light, but this has no basis in fact. For plants to grow evenly, turn them on a regular basis.

To grow good indoor plants, never mix fluorescent and incandescent lights together.

False. An ideal combination involves a balanced light of fluorescent and incandescent fixtures. Plan to have a ratio of one watt of incandescent light for every three watts of fluorescent light. Remember, light intensity drops very rapidly as the distance from the light source increases. For example, if a plant receives about 800 foot candles 6 inches from a light, at 12 inches it would receive only 400; at 18 inches it would receive only about 200 foot candles. Another point is that tubes produce less light as they age. Discard them when the ends blacken or when about ¾ of their life span is used.

Cheaper plant lights are not as good for plant growth as the expensive ones.

There isn't too much difference in growth. The new quartz halogen lights may seem to do a little better, but they are more expensive.

Keeping one's house on the cool side is not good for houseplants.

With some exceptions, most houseplants are comfortable down to 40° or 50°F (4° to 10°C). Plants such as cyclamen, poinsettia, and mums actually prefer it when grown on the cool side, 45°F (7°C) or so. Plants such as African violets do not like temperatures much cooler than room temperature. Certain orchids cannot tolerate low temperatures. Consult a good houseplant book for proper day and night temperatures.

Houseplants will cause windows to sweat, attracting unsightly mold.

Water collects on windowpanes for many reasons. Consider the following:

- ✔ When you mop an 8 × 10 foot (2.5 × 3 m) kitchen floor, you release about 2½ pounds of water, or 2½ pints (1.25 liters).
- ✔ A family of four puts another 12 pints (6 liters) of water a day into the air, simply by breathing and sweating.
- ✔ Cooking dinner for four people adds another 2½ pints (1.25 liters) of water.
- ✔ An electric dishwasher releases another pint.
- ✔ Daily baths or hot showers for four people can add another 2 pints (1 liter).
- ✔ Humidifiers are run in winter to keep our houses from drying out. The person who fills them knows how much water they release.
- ✔ Plants do release moisture. For example, a calceolaria or cineraria houseplant can release 2 quarts (2 liters) of water in 24 hours.

All this moisture condenses on a cold pane of glass (warm inside, cold outside), and surplus water collects, running down on the sill. Greenish mold often finds this a favorable medium to grow on. Actually this moisture is good for humans, even though it does fog up a window. (The problem is worse in modern homes because they are so airtight, shutting out any fresh air.) Fans help control the humidity problem, as do storm windows. Some of the newer windows are so well insulated they do not sweat.

A certain amount of extra moisture benefits the home. It prevents static electricity on your rugs, keeps furniture from cracking, and makes it easier for you and your family to breathe. Plants contribute a small amount of moisture, as well as comfort and pleasure.

Healthy, clean, and shiny leaves can be obtained by using baby oil or leaf shine on the leaves of houseplants.

Baby oil is mineral oil and will clog up the plant's pores, collect dust, and cut down on photosynthesis. Any plant will struggle in these conditions. The best way to get naturally shiny leaves is to wash them with a biodegradable soap (such as Ivory or Safer's).

Stay away from leaf shine products. They do not remove much dirt. They often glue dirt to the leaf, covering it with the shine factor — often silicone. If you want clean, shiny leaves, clean them.

If I keep my houseplants sprayed with an insecticide, we'll never be bothered by insects.

Prevention is generally smart business. Although spraying preventively might keep insects away, it's smarter to wait until you see an insect or two, then zap them. A sound feeding program and regular washing of foliage and stems with slightly soapy water will do more to prevent, deter, and remove insects and eggs than repeated sprayings. When you know you have a slight insect problem, that's the time to hit.

Homemade sprays are not as effective as store-bought sprays for fighting houseplant pests.

False. A new generation of insecticides uses common household ingredients that you can safely mix in your kitchen sink. Here is a formula that is safe around pets and children, and good for the earth.

1. Add 1 teaspoon (5 ml) of liquid detergent (dishwashing type, such as Palmolive, Ivory, or Joy) to 1 cup (250 ml) of cooking oil (such as soybean or safflower), and shake vigorously.
2. Add 2 teaspoons (10 ml) of this mixture to 1 cup (250 ml) of plain tap water and shake again to emulsify it.
3. Pour into a spray or pump bottle. Use this at 10-day intervals, or more often if needed.

This USDA formula is ideal for plants and all kinds of insects. Test the mix on a single leaf first to see if it causes tip burn. You can also buy Safer's Insecticidal Soap, which works fine. A lot of our friends use Murphy's Oil Soap, diluted ¼ cup (60 ml) to a gallon of warm water. Pour this into a spray bottle and spray on plants as needed. (Test any of these on plants first.)

The best way to cope with insects and diseases on your houseplants is to practice "preventive medicine." As soon as you see a pest, crush it before it proliferates into a problem. It takes only a few seconds.

Most holes in leaves of houseplants are caused by insects.

Indoors, most parasitic insects on houseplants such as aphids or mealy bugs (which are sap suckers) can ruin the plant without bothering to make holes in the leaves. Snails and slugs are exceptions along with the caterpillar, but they are rare indoors. "Shotgun" holes in leaves are often a result of bad nutrition or a hot, dry, interior environment. Some plants make their own holes, for example, the Swiss cheese plant *(Monstera deliciosa)*.

If your houseplant is ailing, the best thing to do is take the root ball out and hold it under a faucet, washing away all the soil. Then, put the roots back using a fresh batch of soil.

That's a lot of extra work for nothing, usually. In most cases, what's wrong with the plant is an environmental deficiency (excessive or insufficient light or water, or exposure to extreme temperatures). Unless it's done carefully, removing all the soil from a soil ball could destroy the fragile feeder roots, making it difficult for the already weakened plant to survive this stressful period.

If a houseplant isn't doing well, give it a shot of fertilizer to perk it up.

Fertilizer is not a panacea. Too much fertilizer can burn roots or lead to leaf damage. As the excess salts are carried to the plant, they can accumulate along leaf margins. This can lead to leaf margin and tip burn. Even with the best conditions, recovery of damaged plants may be slow.

If a plant looks sickly and you have fed it within the last two or three months, look for other reasons. Overwatering is the most common cause of plant troubles. Overly dry air in homes or poor circulation can cause leaf and bud drop. Inspect thoroughly for insects. Spider mites are difficult to see — they are almost microscopic. (Fifty of them can do the rumba on the head of a pin.) They cause a yellowish mottling of leaves. To detect, use a magnifying glass or tap the leaves over a piece of white paper.

If I put eggshells, tea leaves, and other kitchen refuse in the soil of my houseplants, it will damage the houseplants.

Go ahead and save all your eggshells, tea leaves, coffee grounds, and other refuse and make up an organic soil mix. Place them in a kitchen can composter, which is nothing more than a 25-gallon plastic garbage can. Add leaves and shredded newspapers to offset odors. This can be placed in a garage where it can slowly break down the materials, giving you a homemade compost without any offensive odors. When the refuse has completely decomposed, you won't be able to recognize any of the original material. Then it's ready to use.

Gelatin is a good fertilizer for houseplants because it contains nitrogen.

Although gelatin contains nitrogen, it's *not* a good fertilizer. In the first place, houseplants need more than just nitrogen to thrive on. Excess nitrogen causes a lot of rapid, weak growth that is highly susceptible to insects and diseases.

Gelatin does not supply nitrogen in the form most easily used by plants, so as a regular fertilizer it's a poor choice. Use one of the many liquid plant foods on the market.

Houseplants do better if they are potbound.

No. Most plants do well without being potbound and some do much better. If you're repotting, shift the soil ball into a pot one size larger and you'll have good luck.

When I repot my houseplants, I like to use a larger pot so I won't have to repot as often.

A lot of people think that if they use an extra large pot, the repotted plant will do better and they will avoid the need to repot for several years. Not so. If you repot, use a pot that is slightly larger. Potting soil in an oversize container can stay too wet when out of the reach of roots for very long. Also, toxic substances may build up and damage the plants.

Clay pots are better for houseplants than plastic or glazed pots.

Clay pots evaporate half the water you give them, directly through the walls of the pot; but glazed pots or plastic types lose no water through the walls. Plants in plastic or glazed containers are more likely to suffer from overwatering, which causes rot. Too much water around the roots shuts out oxygen and causes them to suffocate. Over 98 percent of all air a plant takes in is through the roots.

Remember: Only water plants when the soil starts to dry out — never water when the soil feels moist to the touch.

Green moss on the soil of houseplants is harmful.

Many gardeners are concerned about green moss on the soil surface and pots of houseplants. Sometimes it's so bad you

can smell it. This is due to poor drainage. For houseplants, you can add more perlite or sand to the soil mixture to increase air and water drainage. Also use the tines of a fork to loosen the soil surface. While unsightly, green moss is not harmful but should be regarded as a signal that your soil needs better air and water drainage.

The white crust around the rim, or film on the outside, of clay pots is a fungus growth that can spread to other plants.

False! It's not a fungus growth. What you see are fertilizer and hard-water salts that have oozed through the soil or through the porous wall of clay pots. People who live in a hard-water area often find deposits of calcium and magnesium salts on pots. These salts do little harm, except with succulent plants (such as African violets) whose leaf stems rest on the pot's rim and may get burned. Plastic pots only accumulate this encrustation on the inside rim, not on the outside.

If you find this salt encrustation unsightly, repot the plant. Soak the old pot in hot water with a large dash of household vinegar. Scrub with a wire brush.

Disease and insects kill more houseplants than any other cause.

False! The number one cause of poor performance is excessive water caused by overwatering or poor drainage. For example, a lot of poinsettias do poorly because of too much or too little water. Sometimes the florist's foil holds the water in, causing poor drainage. Leaves curl, turn yellow, and drop. Make sure you don't let houseplants sit in water for more than 24 hours.

If you put pieces of crocks or pebbles in the bottom of a pot, it gives good drainage regardless of soil mix.

False. If the soil mixture has drainage problems, pieces of pots or stones in the bottom may help, but they will not overcome the cause of poor drainage. Replace your soil with a mixture that allows good drainage.

It is unwise to have plants in a bedroom or hospital room because they take oxygen out of the air at night.

During the day, plants give off oxygen necessary for human life. At night, in the absence of light, they do consume tiny amounts of oxygen, but you should not worry about that. Here's why: The air you normally breathe has about 21 percent oxygen. When the atmosphere is less than 16 percent oxygen, you're in trouble. A room 8 × 10 × 10 feet (2.5 × 3 × 3 m) has 168 cubic feet (4.5 cubic meters) of oxygen. If the room contained less than 128 cubic feet (3.6 cubic meters) of oxygen, a person could suffer from an oxygen shortage. During a 12-hour period a human being uses 10 cubic feet (.28 cubic meters) of oxygen; this leaves 30 cubic feet (.85 cubic meters) of oxygen to be absorbed by plants before a shortage could develop.

According to the Agricultural Resource Center at Apopka, Florida, it would take 600 pounds (270 kg) of plants to consume 30 cubic feet (.85 cubic meters) of oxygen. A schefflera 2 feet tall (60 cm) weighs about 3 pounds (135 kg). So, if someone stays in a completely dark bedroom where there is no air exchange for 12 hours, and is packed in with 300 schefflera plants, they might suffer from a lack of oxygen. Only with great difficulty could anyone pack 300 schefflera plants 2 feet tall (60 cm) into a room containing a total of 800 cubic feet (22 cubic meters) of space. Danger would be even more improbable because during the day, those 300 plants would produce more than 150 cubic feet (4.25 cubic meters) of oxygen, if they received light. It is a far greater worry to be in a room where several people are smoking because that process uses up oxygen and gives off carbon monoxide.

When a spider plant *(Chlorophytum)* fails to produce baby spiders, it's because the plant needs a sexual partner.

There is no such thing as a male or female spider plant. Failure to form baby spiders is due to excess artificial light, especially at night. Keep light away from the plant at night and it will produce plenty of plantlets ("spiders") from the flowering clusters.

There is only one true Christmas cactus, and the reason it does not bloom regularly is that it needs a female companion.

A lot of home gardeners feel there is only one holiday cactus — the so-called Christmas cactus. However, there are three holiday cacti: one that blooms around Thanksgiving, one at Christmas, and one at Easter. For show, no plant can rival any of these. The one that blooms in November is the

Thanksgiving cactus *(Schlumbergera truncata)* and is called the "crab claw" or yoke cactus. Look for "sawteeth" that point upward near the ends of its leaves. Also, the leaves of the Thanksgiving cactus are almost twice as wide as the leaves of the Christmas cactus.

There is only one Christmas cactus *(Schlumbergera bridgesii).* It flowers in late December or January and often continues through February and March. Its leaf margins are rounded with scallops along the edges. There are two species of Easter cacti *(Rhipsalidopsis gaertneri* and *Rhipsalidopsis rosea)*, and they start setting buds from January to March. You can tell them by the "cat's whiskers" or bristling hairs at the stem joints or tips. All of these holiday cacti take the same care: soil mixture of equal parts peat moss, perlite, vermiculite, and garden loam. They seem to like to be slightly potbound and can be grown in clay or plastic pots. They all like bright light, filtered or dappled, but not direct sun.

Sex has nothing to do with blooming. The Thanksgiving cactus depends on day length to set blooms. That means no artificial light at night. After buds have formed, it's okay to give light any time. Low night temperature (40° to 50°F, or 4 to 10°C) helps flower buds to form. The Christmas cactus needs more short days and longer periods of coolness than does the Thanksgiving cactus.

The easiest way to get your Christmas cactus to bloom is to leave it outdoors (away from streetlights) in the fall, when night temperatures are cool. Bring it inside before temperatures drop below 35°F (2°C). Easter cacti are not as fussy about day length but like cool temperatures for bud formation.

None will tolerate freezing. You can take cuttings any time of the year. Root them in plain tap water or perlite or vermiculite.

When you buy a cyclamen, get one full of blooms. They last longer.

False. Buy one that's full of buds and has few or no open blooms, so it will last longer. Just two or three blooms on a plant don't have the "wow factor" that more blooms create. As a result, most people pick one with a lot of blooms, which is prettier but shorter-lived. Give your cyclamen plenty of water each day. It prefers a cool window. At night move it to a cool spot, around 45°F (7°C). Pluck out spent blooms and yellowed foliage. After blooming, continue to water the plant and it will bloom for you again later (in about six months).

The only way to encourage a cyclamen to rebloom is to withhold water for several months, then start it up.

The latest wrinkle is this: After your cyclamen finishes blooming, do *not* dry the corm. Continue to water and feed it, and keep it in a bright window. It will bloom eventually, without the usual drying-off period that is often recommended.

The best way to rebloom a gloxinia is to let it go dormant after blooming.

Wrong! Keep it growing by feeding and watering it after it finishes blooming. When gloxinias grow tall and spindly, that means they aren't getting enough light. Although the plants need shade from direct sunlight, too much shade will make them leggy and lanky. Although related to the African violet, they need more light than their country cousins. Gloxinias will grow into well-rounded, bushy plants if turned every two to three days to prevent one side from stretching out farther than the other. Buds that turn brown and never develop (it's called "blasting") are aggravated by too much water, too much plant food, lack of humidity, or a gray mold. The mold is associated with poor ventilation. Sometimes buds refuse to budge. This can be corrected by increasing the humidity around the plant. Or you can set the pot inside a larger pot and pack moist peat moss between the two pots. The moist peat releases enough moisture to prevent buds from blasting or turning brown.

Potted hibiscus makes a poor houseplant because it drops buds faster than it makes them. It grows well outdoors.

Hibiscus makes a good houseplant if you understand it. It will not grow outdoors like the perennial type. There are several reasons for nonflowering: Flower buds develop best when the humidity is high enough to produce strong plants, and when the night temperature is somewhat cool. Full sun is essential. The brighter the window, the more abundant the flowering. It's called an "energy-driven" plant.

In summer, outdoor flowering is almost continuous. Dry-out causes buds to drop and leaves to scorch. These plants have a very strong root system that requires large amounts of water, especially when the plant is outdoors. Soil should be kept slightly moist. When watering a hibiscus in a 6-inch (15-cm) pot, apply enough water so it runs through the pot and into a saucer below. (Note that hibiscus will drop many *leaves* as well as buds if subjected to temperature shock — such as leaving outdoors until nights are in the 40s [°F or 5–10°C].)

A balanced fertilizer works well. It's the phosphorous that encourages flowering. The biggest secret to winter flowering is ample light, and probably the best light source is southern exposure.

Incidentally, this tropical plant is a relative of okra, rose of Sharon, and hollyhock. They all have a habit of setting more buds than they can support, and that's why they shed so frequently. The hibiscus or Rose of China is also called the "shoeblack plant," indicating the use of its flowers by bootblacks in the tropics to polish shoes. The perennial or outdoor hibiscus is *H. moscheutos,* or rose mallow.

Orchids are difficult to grow indoors.

Not true. Some orchids are among the easiest of all houseplants to grow — just be sure to select the easiest. Try the moth orchid, or *Phalaenopsis* ("fail-in-opsis"). It's not only beautiful and easy, but it's easier to grow than the common geranium. Grow it in the kitchen in a well-drained medium such as small pieces of redwood bark. Regular houseplant soil is too dense and will suffocate the roots. It likes warmth, 65° to 70°F (18° to 22°C). Below 50°F (10°C) will kill it. Give it a monthly feeding of a liquid plant food and enjoy its flowers 4 months or so out of the year. We have two *Phalaenopsis* plants on our kitchen table and have flowers almost 6 months out of the year.

Poinsettias and other plants that bloom at Christmas should be put into a closet afterward until November.

Poinsettias and other subtropical plants live where fall days are shorter than summer days. The poinsettia is extremely sensitive to light and darkness. To make it bloom for Christmas, put it on a short-day, long-night schedule starting in September and ending around Thanksgiving. In the subtropics, Mother Nature provides the short days and long nights. But in a lighted living room the plant is likely to get just the reverse, so you should limit its day to about 10 hours and put it to bed for the rest of the night. Even a very dim but continuous light will delay flowering, so a dimly lit hall is not dark enough. Whatever you do, *do not* keep the plant in the dark *both day and night* — just at night, starting at 6 PM and leaving it in the dark until 8 AM the next day. (You can drape a black satin cloth over the plant if no closet is available.)

Is it true that poinsettias are toxic?

Poinsettias are not toxic. The Humane Society no longer warns that they are poisonous to pets, and most poison control centers have taken poinsettias off their toxic plant list. Of course, poinsettia is not a salad plant, and no one should make a meal of it. It is always best to keep pets from chewing on any houseplants unless they are grown for that purpose — such as catnip or catmint.

The number one flowering potted plant sold in the United States is the African violet.

No, it's the poinsettia, a plant that can put on a show way into August or later. Last Christmas, the wholesale value of the poinsettia reached $176 million — a jump of more than 400 percent. Getting these plants to bloom out of their own natural habitat takes a lot of science. It took the combined efforts of the USDA and commercial hybridizers to give us the long-lasting and beautiful varieties we now enjoy.

We're getting lots of letters asking why poinsettias lose their leaves so quickly. This is a sign of poor growing conditions. These tropical plants need at least a half day of sun, a draft-free spot, and a night temperature of about 65°F (18°C). Books say to give the plants a warmer night temperature, but we keep ours in a cool sunroom (55° to 65°F, or 12° to 18°C) and never have any problems. Keep the soil moistened at all times, never soggy or bone-dry. There's a lot of conflicting advice for the poinsettia, but letting the plant go dry or overwatering are reasons for poor luck. We've seen many poinsettias wilt and die because the person failed to punch a hole in the florist's foil to let excess water escape.

2.
Seeds and Bulbs

If you save vegetable and flower seeds over the winter, it produces better plants the following year.

False. The idea that "the older the seed, the stronger the plants" is a real garden myth. The best seed at harvest time will keep the longest in storage, but its vigor *never* increases. Vegetable and flower seeds are at their prime as soon as they reach maximum dry weight on the mother plant.

Seed left over from spring cannot safely be kept for another year. It is not as good as fresh-bought seed.

Leftover seed this year is almost as good as fresh-bought seed last year, if it is properly stored. High moisture, high humidity, and high temperature are the worst enemies of germinating seed.

The best storage for *most* seed is in the refrigerator, not the freezer. Opened foil or any paper seed packets should be placed in a zip-sealing bag. Remove as much air as possible from the bag and seal it tightly before placing it in cold storage. If cold storage is not available, the seed should be stored in a cool, dry environment, such as an air-conditioned office.

Opened packets should be folded down twice and paper clipped, not stapled, to prevent excessive air exchange around the seed. The length of time that seeds remain viable varies greatly, depending on type of plant. Still, it is best to protect the seed from high humidity and high temperatures. Even in a cool greenhouse, seed packets exposed to the sun will get hot and won't last as long.

It doesn't pay to use leftover seed of flowers and vegetables.

If you have some leftover seed, keep in mind that most unused seed remains viable for 2 or 3 years if stored in a cool, dry place in tightly sealed jars with a drying agent ("desiccant") of some kind. Powdered milk is a good material

to store seeds in. Use at a rate of 1 part seed to 1 part powdered milk, and store in a glass jar sealed very tightly. If the
container is moistureproof, many types of seed will remain
viable in a refrigerator for quite some time. The secret is to
keep the seed dry. Lightweight plastic bags are not moistureproof and do not make good storage containers.

Should you collect and save seed from your own garden?

Only if the plants are species, not hybrid. Any hybrid
variety (sometimes marked F_1) yields seeds that will produce
plants with less hybrid vigor and with fewer characteristics of
the hybrid seed originally planted.

If your plants are not hybrids, there is no reason why you
cannot save seed over from year to year and grow your own.
Sometimes that's the only way you can perpetuate the species. Commercial seed vendors may not handle the variety
you like, and often you cannot buy old-fashioned or heirloom
varieties.

Freezing doesn't damage seeds.

If the seeds are not dry enough, water expands and collapses
cell walls. However, if seeds are dry enough for storage (less
than 8% seed moisture), they can be stored in liquid nitrogen
(*that's* cold — minus 197°C or minus 322°F).

In any given batch of seed, the size of the seed makes no difference when it comes to vigor.

For years we've known that large-sized seed of any batch has
more vigor than small-sized seed, if everything else is equal.
Large seed not only germinates more quickly than its smaller
brothers, but produces more vigorous seedlings and can more
readily push through a soil surface. Faster germination and
more vigorous seedlings mean higher yield at harvest. The

reason is that larger seed contains a larger reservoir of food. Some growers order smaller seed because they believe they get more seeds and more plants. If growing conditions are not ideal, this could be a "penny-wise and pound-foolish" idea.

Better germination of seed results when flower and vegetable seeds are planted "face up."

False. This idea probably originated from the fact that bulbs should be planted with the root end down, so the tip can sprout and grow properly. Old-time gardeners always plant lima bean seeds on edge, regardless of whether the eye is up or down, because in this position the seed can rotate easily once it sends down a root and gains leverage. In good soil, even "eye-up" plantings of limas are of dubious value because such soil offers little resistance to sprouts. Most gardeners and commercial growers pay no attention to which side is up or down when planting seeds.

It is more important to plant seeds in a loose mixture and not cover them too deeply.

Some flower seeds do not require any cover at all and germinate better when exposed to light. These include ageratum, begonia, *Browallia, Calceolaria,* coleus, cineraria, German violet *(Exacum)*, gloxinia, strawflower, impatiens, feverfew, flowering tobacco *(Nicotiana)*, petunia, primrose, salvia, and snapdragon.

Tulip bulbs can be kept in the basement over the winter and planted in the spring.

Unplanted spring-flowering bulbs seldom do well when planted in spring. In general, spring-flowering bulbs should be planted before the first hard frost in fall. But in all cases, bulbs are better in the ground than on the shelf. Why not pot them up and place them in a cool spot for 8 weeks, then bring them into a warm room and see if they will bloom. At least it's worth a try. Every second you keep them on a shelf, they go downhill.

If you plant bulbs deep enough, they never have to be moved or divided.

False. Bulbs planted deeply need replanting sooner or later because they multiply and compete with each other for nutrients and water.

When bulbs produce large leaves and no flowers, it means that the soil lacks fertility.

False. It's a sign that the bulbs need dividing and replanting. For example, digging up bulbs of daffodils and dividing them every 2 or 3 years gives bigger and better blooms.

You can arrange tulips and daffodils in the same vase without one damaging the other.

False. Daffodils produce a residue in vase water, affecting a number of flowers including tulips. You can reduce the amount of residue and even eliminate it entirely. Place cut daffodils in a pail of water for 16 hours, then rinse the stems with clean water. Do *not* cut the stems again. Add a little activated charcoal to the water to absorb any remaining residue. Put 1 tablespoon (15 ml) of the charcoal powder per quart (liter) of water and stir.

By adding 5 to 7 drops of concentrated household bleach to a quart (liter) of water, you can control the residue.

Tulips should not be cut down until the leaves and stems are completely withered.

We wait until the leaves have yellowed off by one-third, since they don't make much food after that. If tulips have been in the ground for a year, there is no reason why you cannot rebloom them for another year. Plant more bulbs right over them after they've been cut down. We have seen parks that get a big batch of blooms each year by digging up the bulbs and planting new ones each fall.

Don't try to flower the same bulbs in the same spot over 3 years. A few varieties flower year after year without being separated, but most varieties will not do well after the second or third year.

My tulips don't do well at all the second season of bloom. I've been told that lifting the bulbs, storing them for the summer, and replanting them in the fall will improve their performance. Is this true?

This old-fashioned method is more difficult and is generally a lot of bother. It is better to look for those tulips with a natural propensity for repeat performance. Botanical or species varieties and their hybridized strains (for example, *Kaufmannianas* and *Fosterianas*) are generally excellent garden performers and sometimes will even naturalize. Leave them in the ground, nature's best storage place.

Gladiolus bulbs can change color from year to year.

Gladiolus bulbs do not change color, that is, produce flower spikes with different colors. What actually takes place is that the more robust-growing types or varieties in a mixture outlive and outmultiply the weaker-growing types. It's a matter of survival of the fittest. Glads normally come true to color, although you often see color "sports" with smoky shades. When glads produce large flowers one year and very poor ones the next year, this can usually be blamed on corm diseases or thrips, a very tiny insect that affects the buds and blooms.

3.
Flowers

If I plant perennials I won't have to replant anything next year, and my garden won't require so much work.

No one has ever had trouble-free gardening simply by planting perennials. Not only does it require time and effort to cultivate attractive, showy perennials, but it is not done without an investment. It costs quite a bit to fill a garden bed 10 x 10 feet (3 x 3 m) with perennials. The secret to saving money is to start with seeds or small purchased plants. Another way to save on the investment is to root your own cuttings. Start small and use old standbys — such as peonies, irises, delphiniums. We call these "backbone" plants. You can fill in later with annuals or small, low-growing perennials.

When I go into a flower shop and ask for an 'American Beauty' rose, the florist tells me there's no such rose.

When people buy a rose from a florist, they often ask for the 'American Beauty'. No modern rose has equaled its rich fragrance, and none is likely to take its place in sentimental memories of the older generation. Huge bouquets of it were presented to Lillian Russell by "Diamond" Jim Brady to express his love.

'American Beauty' is no longer common in the florist trade, but it should be available at nurseries.

Heirloom plants are inferior to modern hyrids and should not be used.

Not necessarily. Many old-time gardeners like to grow heirloom plants. There are many seed houses that still carry these seeds to encourage the preservation of traditional strains of historic open-pollinated (nonhybrid) varieties of plant material.

Some gardeners have brought seeds from their native homeland, and the germplasm that descended is a link to the past. It's a good idea to grow some of these heirloom seeds and compare them with modern-day varieties.

Cut flowers should not be sent to hospital patients because of dangerous bacteria that may be in the vase.

A short while ago, a research team at the University of Miami Medical School stated that it had found "gram-negative bacteria" in flower vase water. The researchers suggested that flowers be kept away from high-risk patients. Wire services picked this up and flashed it all over America. David Tapli, Professor of Epidemiology at the Medical School, said, "I don't think there's any danger at all to the average patient in the hospital or home. We've no clinical evidence that flowers ever caused an infection."

Dr. George Maillison, Assistant Director of the Bacterial Disease Division, U.S. Public Health Service Centers for Disease Control in Atlanta, agreed. Another doctor said, "There's a greater risk of bacterial infection from some patients' visitors than from flowers." In other words, don't worry about flowers causing infection. None of us lives in a sterile world. Our skin is covered with bacteria. Bacteria in a flower vase do not travel through the air. In order for the patient to be infected, bacteria would have to be transferred directly by contact or by drinking the water out of the vase.

The custom of sending flowers when someone has died is passé.

False. Having been in the commercial business for over a quarter of a century, we have only one answer: Send them! Florists had a friend in Bette Davis. She wanted people to weep and carry on something fierce at her funeral, and she wanted "millions of flowers." She added: "I don't want anyone sending money to any little charity instead of buying flowers."

Many people think flowers are "overdone" and a waste of money. Unless people have requested donations to a favorite organization, who is to say it's a waste of money? What we'd like to see is more flowers for the living. A tiny bouquet to someone who is alive isn't a bad idea!

Commercial floral preservatives do not prolong the life of cut flowers. Neither do homemade preservatives.

False. Commercial preservatives do prolong flower life and are available at most florist shops. Use according to directions. Homemade preservatives work almost as well. Try this: Mix a quart (liter) of equal amounts of warm water with lemonade, or lemon-lime soft drink, and add a teaspoon (5 ml) of chlorine bleach. Use enough of the mixture to cover at least the lower 3 or 4 inches of the stems where the foliage has been removed.

Because the flower can no longer produce its own carbohydrate food sources, the sugar acts as an alternative energy source. The lemon or lime in the soda provides citric acid, which acts as a preservative, and the bleach prevents bacteria from growing in the water. This mixture will also help flowers bloom if buds are not fully opened.

Place containers of flowers in a cool, well-lit area, not in direct sun or near heating or air-conditioning vents, because drafts dehydrate flowers. If a preservative has not been used, the American Horticultural Society recommends changing the water every 2 days.

A few simple practices can almost double the mileage you get from cut flowers. Here are a few tips.

1. Recut the stems before arranging, about 1 inch from the bottom, making an angled cut with a sharp knife.
2. Remove all lower foliage from the stem. This will help prevent bacteria from building up in the water.
3. Fill the vase with warm water. It contains fewer air bubbles than cold water. Air bubbles can get trapped in the stems and block the uptake of cold water to the upper foliage and flowers. Warm water also works best to thoroughly dissolve floral preservatives.
4. Add a floral preservative. It contains substances that prevent bacteria from growing in the vase. Also, it provides an energy source to ensure long-lasting full blooms.

I bought my wife a bouquet of cut flowers in the supermarket. The bouquet had sprigs of fern fronds in it, but on the undersides of the fronds there were millions of black spots. Is that some kind of disease?

No. The black dots are reproductive structures. Ferns are not flowering plants. They do not produce seeds; they produce tiny spores instead. The dots on the undersides of fern leaves arranged in perfect geometrical lines are called "sporangia" ("spore-an-gee-uh"). Each dot is a cluster of spores and is called a "sorus" ("sore-us") — plural is "sori." Take a look at them and you will see the dots are in straight rows. The dots release the tiny spores, which in turn produce new ferns. However, if the little bumps or dots are scattered helter-skelter on the stems as well as the fronds, then these are scale insects, which can be eliminated by spraying with a mixture of 1 teaspoon (5 ml) liquid dishwashing detergent and 1 cup (250 ml) rubbing alcohol in 1 quart (1 liter) of water. This mixture kills aphids, scale, and other bugs.

Flowers aren't just for women anymore.

True. Flowers aren't just for women anymore. Today it's fashionable for a woman to give flowers to a man. In a survey done by the Society of American Florists, 84 percent of the men surveyed said they would like to get flowers from a woman. The figure is even higher (89%) for men aged 30 to 44. The study showed that half the women are already doing it and the majority of men like it.

For gift-giving satisfaction, be aware when filling a woman's order that the colors women like are not necessarily the same that men like. The American Floral Marketing Council found that the most popular colors among women, in order of preference, are: pale pink, pale purple, hot pink, peach, red, and yellow. Men, meanwhile, prefer these colors in this order: red, yellow, pale pink, hot pink, white, and hot purple.

Splitting or pounding the stems of cut flowers such as chrysanthemums and roses makes them last longer in a floral arrangement.

This is a controversy that keeps coming up. For years we used to pound the ends of woody stems such as those on mums, so they would take up water more quickly. Yet there are some growers who maintain that to mash, pound, or split flower stems has no value.

Cutting the stems on a slant each day does a lot to prolong the life of cut flowers. But pounding? We aren't sure even though we've been doing it for the past 40 years. Cutting on a slant increases the surface exposed for water intake. Also, cutting on a slant is a lot easier to do with a jackknife than cutting it straight across. Try it!

Roses grown in Florida or California are not as hardy as those grown in the northern states.

Southern-grown plants are just as hardy as those grown in the North. A 'Peace' rose in the South is exactly the same as a 'Peace' rose in the North. Southern-grown plants will survive if the plants are exposed to "cues" that promote hardiness, namely, gradually shorter days and decreasing temperatures. However, if the plants are brought from the South late in the year without adequate time to acclimate, they could be injured or killed by cold temperatures even if they are genetically identical to plants that have received the environmental "cues" that promote hardiness (shorter days and colder temperatures). A good way to protect roses is to mound up soil around the base of the plant, at least 12 inches (30 cm) high (but don't rob it from another plant). The soil acts as insulation and protects the canes from freezing.

Ever wonder how freezing kills a plant? We used to think that water in a cell froze, forming ice crystals. Not so, according to Cornell University. The water inside the cell does not freeze. It remains unfrozen. Ice crystals form *between* cell spaces. Water is drawn out of the cell, causing the cells to collapse or shrink. The water that remains inside the cell remains unfrozen. The partial removal of water from inside the cell is what is responsible for freezing injury.

Last spring we bought some pink roses. They grew well but they changed colors. What made that happen?

Actually, roses don't change colors. Here's what happens. All roses are commercially budded on understocks such as 'Odorata', 'Dr. Huey', and others. These understocks are vigorous and produce a root system for the top (the cultivated or desirable variety). Sometimes cold winters, insects, disease, or animals will kill off the top section and the understock will take over. These understocks are of various colors and will shoot up and produce flowers entirely different from the ones you were growing. This accounts for the "change." The original rose did not revert; it just died out, allowing the hardy understock to grow up and bloom. Your best bet is to dig up the "wild" plant and replace it with a new one.

Roses last longer on a bush than in a vase.

You can make a rose last three times longer in a vase than on a bush. Roses on the bush bloom and fade relatively fast.

Roses that produce 7 leaflets indicate "wild" or sucker growth.

Don't believe the old idea that roses with 7 leaflets indicate sucker growth. Most of the modern hybrid tea rose varieties will produce leaves of 7 leaflets, although 5-leaflet leaves usually predominate. You'll find that most of our flowering climbers also have 7 leaflets. You can often tell sucker growth by the long, narrow, light green leaflets. Most sucker growth is thornier than regular, budded varieties. It's better to pull out the suckers than it is to cut them.

Once a florist mum has bloomed, it cannot rebloom.

We used to tell people to discard mum plants after blooming, but now Ed Higgin, chrysanthemum product manager for Yoder Brothers, the world's leading breeder of mums, says that you *can* reflower the holiday plant — although it may not be as spectacular as the original flush of blooms.

Chrysanthemums begin to bud and flower in nature only with the coming of fall and shorter daylight hours. Home gardeners can take a tip from commercial growers and trick the pot mum into flowering by creating artificially shorter days for 8 to 10 weeks before flowering is desired.

Once the pot mum has completely faded, cut back the stems halfway and pinch off or remove any remaining buds to encourage new shoot growth. You'll want to pinch back buds (halfway) once or twice more whenever the new shoots reach 4 to 5 inches (10 to 13 cm) tall to create a bushier plant.

Keep the plant watered regularly, and add a water-soluble plant food. After the last pinch, start forcing the plant to flower by placing it in a dark room 13 to 15 hours each night. Do this by completely covering your mum with a cardboard box or black plastic bag. No peeking! It's important that the dark not be interrupted by any light. Give the mum the dark treatment *daily* for about 6 to 8 weeks, or until flower color can be seen in the buds. Temperatures in the darkness should range from 60° to 70°F (16° to 22°C). Flowers may not develop in darkness under lower or higher temperatures. Return the pot mum to a sunny spot in the day. About 8 to 10 weeks after you start the process, your pot mum should be in full flower. You might be able to reflower the pot mum outdoors (if frost doesn't hit). However, the best chrysanthemums for planting outdoors are garden mums, America's most popular perennial.

Note: Outdoor mums are handled differently. Let them die back in winter. Then in the spring, divide the plants, setting out the small divisions around the clump. Discard any woody stems. Pinch the plant back when it is 9 inches tall and continue pinching out the tips, until about the 4th of July. After that, stop pinching. The mums will mature nicely on their own after that point.

Garden mums are best cut back in fall after blooming to encourage the best blossoms the following year.

It's better not to cut them back in fall. Let them go through a winter with stems on. Stems hold up the snow and make a good mulch. Cut the stems back in early spring, and new growth will come up nicely.

All purple loosestrife is harmful to the ecosystem and should not be planted.

True. *Wild* purple loosestrife *(Lythrum salicaria)* is extremely aggressive and will choke up streams and bodies of water, killing off beneficial plants. Very few plants, tame or wild, can compete with its aggressive behavior. But even though the cultivated varieties were once thought to be sterile, they are now known to be able to spread (though not as rampantly as the wild species).

Oriental poppies produce opium.

The Oriental poppy is not the same as the opium poppy. They are greatly different even though they both originated in the Mediterranean region. The Oriental poppy is a perennial (it comes up automatically each year), whereas the opium poppy is an annual (it must be planted each year). The Oriental poppy has no narcotic properties and may be grown anywhere, but cultivation of the opium poppy is strictly controlled in the United States as well as in many other countries.

It's illegal to grow poppies in the home garden because of the drug they contain.

As far as we know only one poppy — the opium poppy *(Papaver somniferum)* — is illegal to grow. It is the juice of its unripe pod that can be processed into opium. Although you can buy seeds for this poppy, law enforcement authorities have the legal right to seize property and prosecute anyone who grows the plant. Still, it is offered for sale in seed catalogs and we know of no one who has gone behind bars for growing it. But why bother growing this one when there are other beautiful annual poppies you can grow without worrying about serving time behind bars?

There is a perennial we can plant in spring and have it bloom all year long.

There's no such thing. If you want a long show you must plant several different kinds of perennials for a succession of blooms. You'll need to plan it so when one fades out, another comes into bloom.

One reason why peony bushes do not blossom is that they do not get pollinated by ants.

Ants are often seen on peony buds, where they collect nectar produced by the developing bud. Peonies do not need cross-pollination by ants or any insect. When they do not bloom it's because of:

✔ Age. It takes 2 or 3 years to bloom.
✔ Dense shade, especially in a dry soil.
✔ Deep planting (the buds or "eyes" should not be planted deeper than 2 inches below the soil surface).
✔ Botrytis or fireblight, two fungal diseases that abort the buds. Cut off any diseased foliage as soon as you see it any time during the growing season. Spray plants with fungicide in spring.

4.
Vegetables

Cultivating your garden two or three times a week helps by letting sunlight into the soil.

False. First, disturbing the soil increases the loss of moisture due to evaporation. Also, there's a lot of biological activity in the soil that likes to be kept moist and dark. For example, earthworms produce "casts" rich in plant nutrients. The healthiest garden soils are those that are not cultivated so frequently.

Planting by the moon affects plant growth.

One sure way to be ridiculed by scientists is to hint at a relationship between the moon and any natural phenomenon. This reaction is strong and long-standing. You might recall that when Johannes Kepler suggested that ocean tides were influenced by the moon, Galileo said he was sorry to hear that such a brilliant man should be so stupid.

In spite of this, a good many old-timers still "plant by the moon." These folks believe plants that bear above ground should be sown during the waxing moon (from new to full), and root crops should be planted during the waning moon (from full to new moon). There have even been studies that seem to prove this is true: In a test in Germany, full-moon plantings were said to yield 50 to 60 percent more than new-moon sowings.

There may be scientific explanations for successful "planting by the moon." Tides occur in all fluids upon the earth but are noticeable only in large bodies of water such as oceans. It's possible that soil moisture could move toward the surface, due to gravitational force, thus increasing its availability to plants.

How about moonlight? Many feel it affects lovers and so perhaps it also affects plants. It's simply sunlight reflected from the lunar surface. Its intensity is 1/5,000th that of sunlight. Moonlight does not provide enough light to generate

photosynthesis, but it could influence the number of days to flowering and other processes affected by day length.

We feel that people shouldn't automatically discount lunar planting. However, lunar planting or harvesting dates are of no practical value if major factors such as moisture and temperature are ignored.

Lead from autos contaminates the soil or the plants in a vegetable garden located along a busy highway.

There is a possibility that airborne lead from autos would contaminate the soil or cause deposits on foliage. Although leaded gasoline was phased out in the 1970s and 1980s, enough lead did settle out of the air over the preceding 50 years to contaminate the soil. But don't let that keep you from putting in a garden. Just have the soil tested first. Contact your Cooperative Extension Service for the nearest testing source. A soil test will tell you if lead levels near roads (or next to old houses with lead paint) are safe for growing vegetables.

Recently, our friend Nina Bassuk of Cornell University found that the more organic matter that was in the soil, the less the plants took up lead. In short, in soils with abundant amounts of decomposed organic matter (such as sawdust, rotted leaves, manure, and compost) the lead uptake was zero, even though lead concentrations in the soil were 3,000 parts per million. That's why it's a good idea to make compost from grass clippings, leaves, and kitchen waste and, once it is well aged, work it into your garden soil.

Leafy vegetables will accumulate more lead from the soil than root vegetables. Four brassicas — broccoli, cauliflower, kale, and collards — are resistant to lead uptake. Leaf deposits (and pesticide residues) can be washed off foliage surfaces with a vinegar/water solution: 1 tablespoon (15 ml) to 2 quarts (2 liters) of water. Some people use a very mild solution of liquid detergent in water. Rinse well afterward, using plain tap water.

**It is impossible to grow vegetables and flowers near a
black walnut tree because the roots poison them.**

Not all plants are affected by walnut poison. You can grow
many fruits, vegetables, and flowers near a walnut tree and
they aren't affected. According to Iowa State University, the
difference between plants that can grow near walnut and
those that cannot depends on their tolerance to the chemical
juglone (5 hydroxy-1, 4-napthoquinone). Juglone is produced
in walnut leaves during the growing season, then it moves
into the root.

Juglone is a strong toxin that may prevent plants from
fully utilizing energy so that the plants cannot meet the
minimum energy level required for life. Juglone is released
from walnut trees in several ways: leaves falling and decay-
ing; nut husks; root leakage and decay; and rain-drip from
the crown. Juglone is poorly soluble in water and cannot
move far in the soil, but only minute amounts are required to
poison some plants.

Plant roots can encounter juglone when they grow within
½ to ¼ inch of walnut roots. Most walnut roots can be found
at a distance of up to two times the crown radius from the
trunk, but some may extend out as far as three to four times
the crown radius.

Here are some plants we find *will* tolerate walnut poisoning: beauty bush, Tatarian honeysuckle, Norway spruce,
common juniper, lilac, mock orange, hawthorn, variegated
euonymus, violet, bleeding heart, Jacob's-ladder, phlox, blue
hydrangea, hosta, tiger lily, daylily, bee balm, foxglove, white
mulberry, black cherry, black locust, multiflora rose, bitter-
sweet, goldenrod, buttercup, and many grasses. Plants to
keep away from walnuts are: pines, birch, hackberry, apples,
basswood, blackberry, domestic grape, tomatoes, potatoes,
and alfalfa.

Other, related trees produce juglone. For example:
English walnut, pecan, shagbark hickory, and butternut
produce juglone that can affect other plants. But these

species produce only a relatively small amount compared to black walnut.

Hot weather is best for growing good vegetables.

Warm weather is good, but there is a limit and many of our vegetables need a cooling period at night to maintain quality. Sweet corn is a good example. The optimum temperature range for corn production is 75° to 86°F (24° to 30°C). The highest quality is reached when day temperatures range from 75° to 86°F (24° to 30°C) and night temperatures average 55°F (13°C). The cool nights are particularly important at harvest time, slowing maturity and extending the period of optimal sugar content and other quality factors in sweet corn.

Watering vegetable plants during the day will kill them if the sun is hot.

Not so, though there are some exceptions such as garden beans. Watering during the day results in the loss of a lot of water to evaporation, about 33 percent — it is pretty wasteful. So do the job in the early morning and allow the leaves to dry off during the day.

It's better to soak your vegetable plants well before harvesting the crop because it makes them juicier.

False. It's better to withhold water from certain vegetables just before harvesting. These include tomatoes, cucumbers, and squash. They have a better flavor if picked after they've gone through a few days of a dry spell. Most of these are already 85 percent water, and if soil moisture is excessive it seems to dilute the flavor. In other words, a dry spell before picking actually enhances the flavor of many of these crops. They also seem to keep a bit longer if picked after a short dry spell. Furthermore, dry weather and low humidity for several weeks before harvesting peaches, nectarines, and plums can help reduce brown rot fungi.

Salt is a good weed killer for asparagus.

The old idea that salt is good for asparagus has been discredited. Tests show that salt is of little value as a weed killer. Yet there are people who want to use salt, and if you're one of them, use the fine grade type (2 pounds per gallon of water, or 0.9 kg per 3.75 liters). Apply when weeds are 3 inches (8 cm) high — but don't be disappointed if the weeds keep on growing.

Small carrots are more tender than large carrots.

Tenderometer and cutting tests have shown that small, slender carrots are not more tender than larger ones.

Old-fashioned corn has better flavor than modern varieties.

No doubt about it, we believe that the eating quality of our new high-sugar hybrids is clearly better than the old varieties. The new sweet corns have superior flavor in a full range of maturity dates. The old-fashioned sweet corn varieties are what is known as "open pollinated." These are different from the new hybrids because the corn comes true from seed year after year. A lot of people still prefer them, even though little improvement work has been done on them since the advent of hybrid sweet corn back in the 1930s.

Gourmet cooks use a special variety of corn called "baby corn" or "finger corn" that's only 2 inches (5 cm) long.

There's no such variety of baby or finger corn (as of this writing). The "baby" corn is just immature ears of sweet corn, or even field corn (used for feeding cattle). No special variety of corn is needed. Just plant your corn seed rows close together (6 inches, or 15 cm apart) and harvest the tiny corn ears when the silks start to emerge from the husk leaves. Tiny cobs will be about 3 inches long with perfect but barely developed kernels. The fingerlike ears are entirely edible and delicious for hors d'oeuvres, stir fries, and pickles.

Recently there has been word that seedsmen are producing a silkless baby corn.

Whenever we grow corn, the ears get an ugly black boil on them. Also, I heard there are corn varieties that do not get this condition, and that the boils can cause cancer.

Those black patches or boils on ears and stalks are corn smut, which is worse in hot weather. When the soil is dry, the dust blows more readily and it is by means of airborne dust that the powdery fungus spores are carried from one garden to another.

There is no one variety that is immune to corn smut, and there is no chemical control. Pick the boils and burn them as they appear. Get your neighbors to do the same.

There is no evidence that corn smut causes cancer. And although most gardeners take great pains to eradicate the deadly corn smut, others are actually growing it for human food. Some U.S. mushroom companies grow and distribute the fungus *(Ustilago maydis)*. David Pope, president of a mushroom company, has sold hundreds of pounds of smut — grown with a special technique that treats the corn at just the right maturity — at about $10 per pound. The delicacy has a smoky mushroom flavor (the corn taste does come through) and is most popular at Mexican restaurants.

Most gardeners remain convinced that smut is not worth growing. The fungus matures so fast, it's usually overripe by the time it's spotted in a corn patch.

The only sure way to have sweet corn on the table is to pick the corn and cook it immediately in boiling water.

Gourmets used to say you should have the water boiling before you go out to pick sweet corn, but this is now whimsy. Some new corn varieties with 25 percent more sugar hold their sugar content for hours. If new corn varieties are kept refrigerated, they will lose little sweetness for several hours after picking. Growers for quality roadside stands pick in the cool of the morning and keep corn cool in the sales area. The husks should not be removed before refrigeration.

Here's our method: Picked ears (husks left on) are placed standing up in a shallow pan of water (2 or 3 inches deep). Husks are sprayed with water and then the pan is set in a shady spot, until time for eating.

Cucumbers can be crossed with muskmelons and watermelons, but this gives them a bad flavor.

Cucumbers do not cross with muskmelons, watermelons, pumpkins, and squash. Different varieties of cucumbers will cross-pollinate, however. Even if they do, the edible portion will not be affected.

Nubbins and crooks are the result of improper pollination. That's why you shouldn't move the vines any more than necessary while cultivating or picking. Moving the vines destroys blossoms, drives away bees, results in kinking and matting of the vines, and tends to increase the number of misshaped fruits.

Flat, tasteless melons can be due to a lack of magnesium or boron in the soil. It has been found that such fruits can be sweetened by giving the vines a dose of Epsom salts and borax. For home gardens, use about 6½ tablespoons (98 ml) of Epsom salts and 3½ tablespoons (50 ml) of borax (household type) to 5 gallons (19 liters) of water. Spray the plants when the vines start to run, and again when the fruits are between 1 and 2 inches (2.5 to 5 cm) in diameter.

Garlic contains a material that can affect your voice tone, making you sound hoarse.

Garlic can actually improve your voice. Colm Wilkinson, the Irish tenor in the Broadway hit *Les Misérables,* protects his voice for his strenuous 3 hours onstage by chewing half a clove of garlic each night.

In our day, a teacher sometimes sent a child home from school because he or she reeked of garlic. Today, garlic is widely accepted and used.

Garlic keeps best in a cool refrigerator.

False. Garlic keeps best in an airy spot, where the temperature is around 60° to 65°F (16° to 18°C).

The only way to get garlic breath is by eating it.

You can get garlic breath just by handling lots of the bulbs. An often-cited experiment found that garlic rubbed into the feet of a 12-year-old boy later tainted his breath. Aromatic substances in garlic seem to enter through the pores, arrive in the bloodstream, and get released in the lungs, where they are exhaled. When you eat garlic its aromatic components go from the bloodstream to the lungs, which is why you can't always get rid of the odor simply by brushing or rinsing. The same is true of other aromatic foods such as onions and curry. The aromatic features of these foods can come out through your pores.

It takes about 24 hours for the aroma to dissipate from the bloodstream. The best approach is to mask the odor by chewing peppermint, wintergreen, or parsley. These follow the same metabolic route as garlic, releasing pleasant aromatic substances through the lungs. Gargling with a teaspoon (5 ml) of baking soda in a glass of water will help in absorbing the unpleasant odors, just as baking soda does in your refrigerator.

Poisonous mushrooms (or toadstools) found in lawns or gardens will turn a silver spoon black.

The old idea that only poisonous mushrooms will turn a silver spoon black is dangerous and false. We're often asked how to tell if mushrooms are toxic or not. This is one sector of horticulture we don't give advice on because some deadly mushrooms look very much like the edible types, and there is no antidote for poisonous mushrooms. Probably about 90 percent of mushroom deaths are caused by eating the Amanita or "death cap." Unless you're trained in the field, our advice is to avoid eating any mushroom growing wild.

All hot peppers have the same amount of heat. It's the way you grow them and cook them that makes the difference.

False. Some peppers are naturally hotter than others. Habañero ("ah-ben-yarrow") is the hottest, based on Scoville Heat Units. This is a rating scale for the heat of hot peppers. Here's how several selected chile peppers rate.

Scoville Rating

Pepper Type	Scoville Heat Units
Habañero	200,000–300,000
Carolina Cayenne	100,000–105,000
Tabasco	30,000–50,000
Chile pequin	40,000
Cayenne	35,000
Chile de arbol	15,000–30,000
Serrano	7,000–25,000
Hungarian wax	2,500–6,000
Jalapeño	3,500–4,500
Ancho/poblano	2,500–3,000
Anaheim, New Mexico chiles	250–1,400
Bell	0

Source: Ben Villalon, Texas A&M University

My husband has been hooked on hot peppers. He eats them even though it makes him cry. Is it true they are addictive?

It is true. Hot peppers are mildly addictive, but it's a safe addiction. They stimulate the production of endorphins, the same mood-enhancing morphinelike painkiller that produces a "runner's high."

If you want to grow really hot peppers in your garden, try the 'Scotch Bonnet', or 'Habañero'. It's the hottest pepper in the world.

The main reason why pepper plants will not set fruit is that the soil is too rich, causing "all bush and no bloom."

Soil fertility has little to do with fruit setting, although fertilizer can affect production. A balanced rich soil yields good peppers. But too much nitrogen in the soil stimulates lots of leaves at the expense of fruits — though that alone would not prevent *all* fruit production.

When pepper plants do not set peppers, blame it on the weather or atmospheric conditions. A hot drying wind at the time of bloom will cause buds and flowers to drop. Variety has a lot to do with fruit set. If you live in an area with a short growing season, use a pepper that has been bred for the area.

You should plant pepper plants close together so they can pollinate one another.

Each pepper plant has its own male and female flowers and does not need another plant for cross-pollination.

We read the report that hot chile peppers can cause cancer in humans. The article linked stomach cancer to chile pepper eating.

You are speaking of a study that was flawed from the beginning and has been disputed by the medical community all over the world. If you really want the facts, look in the October 1994 issue of *Chile Pepper* magazine. It exposes the bogus chile cancer scare. Let's not deprive "Chile-heads" (including us) of the pleasure of eating hot peppers.

Every year we have a lot of peppers but they are all green. We're told that's because we never bought red pepper seeds or plants.

False. Red peppers are just ripe green peppers. The red pigment is masked by the green pigment (chlorophyll). There are several reasons why the green ones won't turn red:

✔ **Variety.** Some varieties turn more quickly, for example, 'La Bamba' and 'Canape', both sweet elongated peppers. Their walls are not as thick and thus turn red faster.
✔ **Soil type.** A sandy dry soil will cause peppers to turn red more quickly than a watersoaked clay soil.
✔ **Mulch.** A black plastic mulch will heat up the soil and hasten reddening, whereas an organic mulch will delay reddening because it cools the soil.
✔ **Weather.** Hot, dry winds will cause the blossoms to shed. New blossoms will set later, and if you do not have a long growing season the fruits do not get a chance to mature and turn red. If you have a long growing season and frost doesn't come early, the fruits will mature. If the new fruits form later they may not get enough good weather to develop; that's one main reason why you get a lot of green peppers, instead of red ones.

When popcorn doesn't pop, it's because the seed is old and dead.

Not so. If popcorn isn't popping well, it means the kernels have lost moisture. Steam makes the popcorn pop. Put new life in kernels by placing them in a quart (liter) jar filled about ¾ full, seal, and place in the refrigerator. If they still don't pop, add 1 tablespoon (15 ml) of water per quart (liter) jar, and reseal. Shake the jar at least twice a day. Sealed glass jars kept in a refrigerator keep popcorn good for several years. Popcorn, if left in open containers, can lose ½ percent moisture in 24 hours. Take it out of plastic bags and keep it in air-tight jars.

Potato skins served in restaurants contain a toxic material.

Since both of us came from potato farms, we must admit we're fond of potatoes. And the best part of a baked potato is the crispy, crunchy skin. Tests show that both peeled and unpeeled potatoes are not only safe to consume, they are a gold mine of nutrients. Baked or fried, skins should be eaten because ounce for ounce the skin has far more fiber, iron, potassium, and B vitamins than the flesh. It is true that cooked potatoes do contain a small amount of glycoalkaloids, natural plant toxins that repel insects and predators. Every cooked spud contains a small amount of the toxin, mostly in the peel.

Some nutritionists say you should peel potatoes before cooking them. They say that growers use a mildly toxic chemical to keep potatoes from sprouting in storage. Regardless of how you bake, boil, pressure cook, or microwave potatoes, traces of the sprout inhibitor linger in the skins. On the potato farm, the only warning we knew was: Don't eat potatoes with a green skin because green potatoes contain more alkaloids.

The human body is a great metabolizer. It can dispose of the sprout inhibitor that remains on the skins. You would have to eat four large potatoes to get even close to the full amount of natural toxins and sprout inhibitor (CIPC) the Environmental Protection Agency says is unsafe to consume. How about the gobs of gravy or sour cream some people shovel on? To us, the fat in these ingredients poses health risks that could dwarf those of the skins.

There is a nutritional difference between red and white potatoes.

The Potato Board tells us there is no measurable difference between the two. Both types provide the same amount of vitamins C and B, potassium, thiamin, iron, and dietary fiber. Potatoes are a great bargain, but many people do not eat them because of the misconception that they are fattening. Actually the spud is 80 percent water, about the same as milk. It's the stuff you put on the spud that makes the calories. Instead of butter or sour cream, try lemon juice or chive-spiked yogurt on baked or boiled potatoes.

Don't refrigerate potatoes. Below 40°F (4°C), they develop a sweet taste as starch changes to sugar. This increased accumulation of sugar will cause the potatoes to darken when cooked.

Pumpkin pies are always made of pumpkins.

Many so-called pumpkin pies are made from the large squash *Cucurbita maxima,* which can be grown in any garden. One variety is 'Golden Delicious' and another is 'Blue Hubbard'.

Squash makes a better pie, with thicker consistency, brighter color, and more flavor. Some canners mix pumpkins with squash, but federal laws insist the proportions be labeled.

Our modern tomatoes are less acidic than older varieties, so they pose a health hazard in home-canning due to the danger of botulism.

Our modern varieties are no less acidic than varieties grown previously. The USDA and various state colleges tested nearly 200 varieties to arrive at this conclusion. A news release from the USDA stated: "Contrary to what you may have heard, the tomato varieties grown in the U.S. today are actually just as safe as the old-time varieties." The so-called low-acid tomatoes are actually not low in acid, but high in sugar. The sugar masks the tart flavor of the tomatoes.

However, all tomatoes qualify as nonacidic foods; and nonacidic foods, if not processed long enough, are subject to botulism growth in sealed containers. If you use good canning practices such as a pressure cooker or hot water bath, and process them for the recommended length of time, there should be no problem. Avoid using overripe fruit or produce with spots. These could introduce organisms that might lower the acidity. If a can is improperly sealed or if you find mold on it, discard the contents and boil the jar.

Pink, white, and yellow tomatoes are less acidic than red tomatoes.

They all have the same amount of acidity, but the pink ones have more sugar in them, and that masks the acidity. Usually many of the large "beefsteak" tomatoes are pink. For example, there's a variety called 'Ponderosa Pink' that's listed as a beefsteak type. Then there's a 'Pink Girl Hybrid' that is resistant to tobacco mosaic, verticillium, and fusarium wilts.

You don't get good yields from tomato plants unless you prune them.

There are people who prune and those who don't. People who do not prune get good crops. We'll try to explain pruning. You will note that as your plant grows, shoots appear in the axils of the leaves (where the leaf attaches to the stem). These shoots are called "suckers" and should be removed when 2 to 4 inches long. They can be pulled off easily by grasping the sucker with the thumb and forefinger, and pulling outward and downward.

If you remove the suckers with a knife, be sure to sterilize it with a bleach solution in between plants so you don't transmit viral diseases from one plant to another. Should the suckers get away from you and reach a length of a foot or more, you can still remove them without causing too much injury to the plant — but it's best to remove them while they are small.

About the time you start picking your first tomatoes, it might be advisable to discontinue pruning or suckering the plants. Allow the late suckers to grow and provide shade for the 5 or 6 "hands" (flower clusters) of tomatoes below. But if pruning sounds too complicated, then forget the job! You can grow all the tomatoes you want without resorting to any pruning whatsoever.

What's the best seedless tomato?

There is no such thing as a seedless tomato in nature, but there are tomatoes that have fewer seeds than others. Quite often the beefsteak and plum-shaped tomatoes have fewer seeds, but they all have seeds.

If you can't eat tomato seeds, you can use a hormone spray such as Blossom-Set that will ripen tomatoes 1 to 3 weeks earlier. Most of these tomatoes will ripen before they set seeds because the fruit will be set by chemicals, not by pollen.

You can buy these hormones in any garden center. Apply early in spring when temperatures go below 60°F (16°C) or as the first or second "hands" are blooming. Spray the flower clusters when they are open or partly open. We spray the flower clusters as soon as two or more blossoms are open, with repeated spraying weekly to set flowers opening later.

Tomato flowers often fail to set fruit and will drop off the plants, especially in the early part of the season, due to cool nights (below 59°F or 15°C) or short, cloudy days and lack of sunlight — all conditions unfavorable for pollination. The hormone spray makes the fruit set despite poor weather.

There is a story that Robert Gibbon Johnson ate the first tomato in America, in front of an astonished audience in Salem, New Jersey. Women fainted, expecting him to froth at the mouth from eating the "deadly" vegetable.

The credibility of this myth should be viewed about one step above the tooth fairy fable. The Johnson story is perhaps the most popular "tomato introduction" tale, but there are over 500 known stories about who first produced and consumed this wondrous fruit in North America. Perhaps the most famous and earliest attribution was published in 1825 by Thomas Jefferson, who credited London-born Dr. Sequeyra with introducing the tomato to North America during the mid-eighteenth century.

Robert Gibbon Johnson did in fact exist and lived in Salem. Beyond that, there is no other historical evidence to support the tomato myth for which he is famous. We'll settle it once and for all here: Prior to September 26, 1820, Americans considered the tomato to be poisonous. Robert Gibbon Johnson, who was one of Salem's most prominent citizens, imported seeds from South America and planted them in his garden. When they ripened he intended to eat their fruit on Salem's courthouse steps, so the story goes . . . an eloquent myth.

Enjoy tomatoes. They're America's number one vegetable. (After many years of controversy, the U.S. Supreme Court decided the tomato is a fruit that is treated as a vegetable.)

A sunny window is the best place to ripen green tomatoes.

Tomatoes do not need light or high temperature to ripen. The best temperature to ripen green tomatoes is about 58°F (14°C). At this temperature, color development will occur slowly and the fruit will keep the longest. Each can be wrapped in a piece of newspaper. This helps confine ethylene gas, which is given off by all fruit and hastens ripening. When tomatoes are bright red, they can be stored in the refrigerator but refrigerating them before they are fully ripe can impair taste.

You can graft a tomato onto a potato (or vice versa) and get a "pomato," bearing tomato fruit above and potato tubers below.

False. "Pomato" is supposed to be a freak produced by grafting a tomato shoot (scion) onto a potato rootstock. Some mail-order companies have advertised that a pot they sell will produce a "pomato," bearing tomato fruit above and potato tubers below. Professor R.W. Robinson, a vegetable specialist at the New York State Agricultural Experiment Station in Geneva, New York, tells us this is nothing more than a potato tuber and a few tomato seeds planted in the same pot. It will produce a low yield of both tomatoes and potatoes as advertised, but on separate plants.

In a laboratory you can produce a hybrid between a potato and a tomato by tissue culture (protoplast fusion), but the hybrid will be sterile. In nature, tomatoes do not cross with peppers or potatoes.

Tomato and pepper plants can be cross-pollinated.

Impossible. Tomatoes and peppers are in the same family (Solanaceae) but of different genera and cannot cross-pollinate. The pepper-like tomatoes are simply puffy tomato fruits. A variety called 'Pepper' is available that looks like a bell pepper, and is often stuffed and baked like a pepper. In other words, it's a stuffing tomato. The fruit has large air spaces in it, and sometimes the fruit is elongated somewhat like a jalapeño pepper.

Is it possible to grow good tomatoes from hybrid seeds you collect?

You'll have some good plants, but nothing like the parents whose seed you saved. We'll explain. Your plants were all F_1 hybrids, "first-generation" parents. If you save seeds from these F_1 hybrids and plant them, you no longer have the hybrid quality. Seeds collected from fruits of F_1 hybrids will not produce a plant of the same caliber as the parent. Qualities such as disease resistance and other hybrid characteristics may be lost if seed is saved and sown. That doesn't mean you won't get good plants and good fruit, however; but don't expect it to have all the hybrid strong points. Let the seed companies produce hybrid seed.

The more you cultivate around tomatoes and other vegetables, the more vegetables you'll have because it keeps weeds down.

False. More than any other single fact, it is improper cultivation that causes tomatoes to produce below their potential. Close weeding injures the root system. Your best bet is to soak the plants well and apply a mulch such as straw, newspapers, or plastic to trap moisture inside and to cut down on water-robbing and nutrient-robbing weeds. Mulches reduce fruit-cracking and blossom-end rot, common problems with tomatoes.

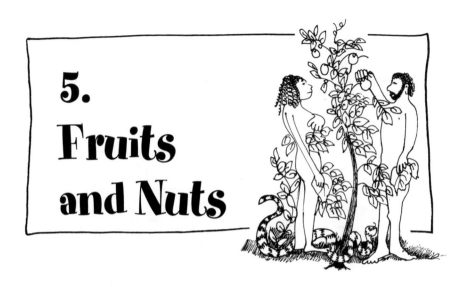

5.
Fruits
and Nuts

The best way to tell if a watermelon is ripe is by thumping it with your knuckles.

Thumping is a poor way to tell whether a watermelon is ripe. A better method is to check the color where the melon has rested on the ground. When ripe, those melons that are predominately dark green, such as 'Crimson Sweet', 'Congo', or 'Black Diamond', will turn a buttery yellow on the ground side. Lighter melons such as 'Charleston Gray' will also turn yellow, but not as deep as the darker varieties, when ripe.

Another change that takes place is that the color becomes dull when the fruit is ready to pick. This method of detecting ripeness will require some practice, but when it is mastered, it will give you the optimum sugar content and the firmest flesh possible.

You can tell a ripe muskmelon by shaking it close to your ear.

This technique actually tells you nothing. The noise you hear is not quality, but rather loose seeds. The best guide to quality in buying, as in picking, is the condition of the netting on the fruit, the color of skin, and resilience. On a muskmelon, the netting should be coarse and the rind showing through should be gray-yellow. A ready-to-eat melon will feel springy when slight pressure is applied.

The best time to pick cantaloupes is when the ends are soft.

The time to pick cantaloupes is when the body color turns to a yellowish-green. Don't test the skin with your fingernail, as rot may set in. Rather, try the "half-slip" method, which is quite reliable. Press lightly on the stem with your thumb at the point where the stem joins the fruit. If the disc slides off with just a little resistance, the melon is ready. Cantaloupes don't develop additional sugar after they are picked. If taken from the vine too green they will never become sweet, though they will soften. Honeydew melons have a sweet odor when ripe, and a yellowish color to the skin.

Melons that have netting on the outside skin have a better flavor than melons without a netting.

False. You can have a high-quality melon with very little netting.

You can tell the ripeness of an orange by its skin color.

No, you can't judge an orange by its color. If you look at an orange in the backyard of a Florida resident, it'll look greenish but still be ripe and juicy. The Florida Department of Citrus is trying to dispel the notion that a ripe orange must have orange skin. American consumers "buy with their eyes" and that's why oranges are artificially colored. The Florida growers have a campaign to eliminate this practice of coloring. No oranges are picked before they are mature regardless of whether the skin is bright orange or completely green. Cooler night temperatures set the orange color. Oranges from warmer areas tend to be greener. Retailers like to get colored oranges because they look better on shelves. Not all Florida oranges are artificially colored, and we like them just as well.

A nectarine is a cross between a peach and a plum.

False. A nectarine is simply a fuzzless peach. Technically, the genetic character of the nectarine is non–fuzz bearing.

The pits (seeds) from home-canned peaches are toxic and could kill you.

Not necessarily. My mother often canned peaches whole because the kernels (pits) imparted a delightfully nutty flavor. Compounds containing cyanide are found in some fruit pit kernels and in some other foods as well. Even cabbage, broccoli, and cauliflower (called "cancer fighters" today) contain cyanide but not enough to make them unsafe to eat. Many fruit pits contain cyanide. Apricot seeds, for example, contain a compound called "amygdalin," the supposedly active ingredient in laetrile, the discredited cancer drug. No doubt the almonds you buy in stores also contain cyanogenic glycosides that are broken down into cyanide by enzymes in your body.

Studies of peaches and apricots show that 13 to 15 raw peach pit kernels could get you into the lethal cyanide range for adults, according to Dr. M. Dietert of Cornell University. For children, about 15 percent of the adult level could be lethal. Apple seeds contain cyanide, about ¼ as much as peach pits by the same weight. Although they are very small as compared with peach kernels, eating a cupful of apple seeds has caused cyanide poisoning. Eating a couple of seeds is not a problem, although we've known several people who actually loved eating apple seeds — a dangerous practice.

Driving nails into a fruit or nut tree will make it bear.

False. Trees do not need iron to bear fruit. In any case, they cannot absorb it from a nail.

If you pound the trunk of a nut tree with a club, it will cause the tree to bear.

Nut trees that fail to bear nuts will not be helped by beating; bruising trunks only invites disease. Bad weather at pollination time may prevent blooms from being fertilized. Searing winds can also prevent pollination. The age of the tree is

important, too. Some nut trees will not bear until they are 10 to 12 years old. Shade and competition from other trees can be another cause of nonbearing.

You can grow fruit trees from seeds or pits that will turn out to be just as good as nursery-bought stock.

False. You can start trees from seeds and pits, but the chances for getting edible fruit are slim. What you could get in most cases is "common" or bitter fruit. It's possible to start a peach tree from a pit and get very tasty peaches sometimes. But in most cases the fruit will be hard and lack flavor. Birds and other animals start many apple trees from seed (they eat the fruit and expel the seed). The seed produces a wild apple, but only in rare cases is edible fruit produced. Johnny Appleseed started a lot of apple trees from seed (collected from cider mills); although some of his trees may have produced edible fruit, in most cases the fruit was "wild" or "common."

You can start seeds from oranges and grapefruit and get plants that flower and even bear fruit, but expect the fruit to be sour.

Nurserymen start fruit trees by budding and grafting. They use material produced by tissue culture and graft or bud it onto wild rootstock, and it will grow into a tree with edible fruit.

It is impossible to grow apples clean enough to eat in the dark without spraying them heavily.

A lot of organic gardeners are doing it. Here's a good tip from a reader of our column: Make a solution of 1 cup (250 ml) vinegar, 1 cup (250 ml) sugar, and 1 quart (1 liter) of water. Mix well and pour into a plastic gallon jug. Leave the cap off. Hang the jug in an apple tree. No more wormy apples. This really works on Northern Spy and other varieties in our yard.

One of the more vexing fruit-blemishing diseases of home orchardists is apple scab. This fungal disease infects leaves and fruit starting in early spring, and then during periods of rainfall continues to spread on the tree for the remainder of the growing season. Most popular apple varieties grown include McIntosh, Delicious, Cortland, and Empire — all susceptible to scab. To grow edible fruit on these trees it takes numerous and timely chemical fungicide doses.

Fortunately, there is an alternative to growing "scab-prone" apples: Plant disease-resistant varieties. These scab-resistant apple varieties still need management of insect pests. Although not altogether "foolproof," including these apples in the home orchard should make harvesting doubly rewarding, as the crop will be produced with minimal pesticide impact. Other disease-resistant apples include Liberty, a fine dessert apple with tart-sweet flavor. Prima has attractive, red-orange skin with yellow-green background color.

6.
Trees
and Shrubs

You shouldn't prune bare-root stock or balled and burlapped trees when transplanting.

Based on our 30 years of nursery work, we think you should prune back the top at least one-third to compensate for root loss during digging. It's known that 98 percent of the roots are lost when a tree or shrub is dug. That means the remaining 2 percent of roots have to nurse the same top, unless you trim it back at least one-third.

The best treatment for a tree that oozes liquid is to insert a drainage tube.

First, your tree has bacterial wet wood. Inserting a drainage tube was once commonly done, but it has now fallen into disfavor and rightfully so. The tube is supposed to relieve pressure, but since you cannot see inside a tree you can't find out where the pressure is. Many arborists tell us that drilling breaks down the tree's natural defense boundary, thus allowing disease organisms a potential entry into healthy wood. So, most arborists argue against the drainage tube treatment. Most trees affected by bacterial wet wood are healthy despite the unsightly, sometimes malodorous ooze. There is some evidence that wet wood may actually lubricate tight branch crotches, thus helping to prevent or minimize breakage. So, the best advice today is this: Do nothing.

Some people say you should paint a tree dressing on a wound left where a limb was cut off, and others say not to put any kind of a tree dressing on.

This is one of those things everyone will never agree on, but the latest thinking is that dressings are not needed on tree wounds. If you'll notice, apple growers who prune off limbs do not treat the wounds. Exposure to air seems to favor callusing and they let it go at that. In fact, quite often the dressing applied does more harm than good because some dressings break away from the wood, leaving a space for insects, fungi, and bacteria to work. In most cases, tree wounds will become closed by a natural callus — without any aid. Of course, that doesn't mean the tree is healed completely, because decay may have started and may continue to grow into the sapwood and heartwood.

Dr. A.L. Shigo of the USDA Forest Service and Dr. C.L. Wilson of Ohio Agricultural Resource Center made an extensive study of wound dressings.

Their tests included more than 400 wounds deliberately made on shade trees; after 5 years they found that the wound dressings had no effect on the rate of healing, and the dressings failed to prevent infection by wood decay fungi. The least decay occurred in the untreated wounds. These two men concluded that their tests "point out the fallacy that dressings protect against wood-inhabiting microorganisms."

It's impossible to get a potted Christmas tree to live after it's been in the house.

False. The practice of buying and using a living tree for Christmas is increasing, but it can be tricky. Keeping an evergreen growing in good health takes a little doing. First, many of the roots (about 98%) were left behind when the tree was dug. If the tree is growing in a container, it probably will be less at risk than if it is balled and burlapped. Don't take the tree indoors until the last minute. After all, the temperature indoors runs 72°F (22°C) or more, and humidity 12 percent or less. Keep it in the heated house only a few days, 4 or 5 at the most. If it stays indoors too long, it may lose its resistance to freezing temperatures. Also, we've seen new growth start indoors, and that new growth is quite vulnerable to damage when the tree is taken outdoors.

It's a good idea to adjust the tree gradually to the change in temperature when taking it indoors, and again when returning it outdoors.

Make sure a hole is dug outdoors well in advance. After Christmas, take the tree out of the pot carefully, set it in the hole, and water it well on warm days. It's even a good idea to loosely wrap burlap around it to shelter it from the sun and wind.

Look for a small tree with a large root ball, rather than a large tree with a small root ball. The best kinds of trees to buy at Christmas are Douglas Fir or Concolor Fir. They are smaller, they grow fast, and they have less chance of dying.

When you prune off a limb on a tree, you should make the cut flush to the trunk.

False. The old idea of cutting flush to the trunk injures the collar of the branch. This, in turn, causes damage within the trunk. So, when you prune, leave a little collar instead of cutting off the limb flush.

A tree should be planted facing the same direction it was in the nursery.

We've asked a lot of good growers about this and have come to this conclusion: There's no point in planting the tree in the exact same position it grew in the nursery. We asked Bill Flemer III of Princeton Nurseries. He concurs: "We ourselves have done experimenting in years gone by to see whether tree orientation has any effect on success in transplanting. The results were entirely negative. Fussing with trunk orientation merely adds to the contractor's expenses and provides no significant benefit for survival and growth of trees."

He adds: "There are a few landscape architects who make a big fuss on this matter and carefully mark the south side of the tree so that it can be planted with that side again facing south. There is no significant benefit to this."

Trees that have cavities should be filled to prevent decay.

False. Filling cavities often causes more damage to them. Cavities develop slowly following severe wounding. A small cavity has little effect on trunk or branch strength, but when the cavity diameter reaches about two-thirds of the trunk or branch diameter, caution is advised. If you must fill a tree cavity, say for cosmetic reasons, don't use hard materials such as cement, asphalt, or rocks, which will gouge the inside when the tree moves in the wind. Such materials also speed up the decay process. Draining of cavities is not recommended because drain holes provide entryways for decay organisms and because water-soaked wood is likely to decay more slowly than well-aerated wood. In the long run, prevention of cavities is the answer.

Tree roots have the ability to seek out water sources no matter how near or far away.

Roots cannot seek out moisture. During dry periods, the water table recedes due to the lack of replacement moisture. Therefore, you should water trees during extended dry periods.

When a tree is planted, it should be wrapped to prevent frost cracks and to keep out the sun and insects.

More often the tree is killed by the tree wrap itself. Even cotton twine may not rot fast enough to keep from girdling a small tree. If the string is not removed, the tree may be girdled and die. Tree wrap is an excellent place for disease and insects to thrive.

Hardware cloth (screen) around the base of fruit trees will prevent girdling by rabbits, voles, and other animals. If you use a tree guard (invented to keep horses from nibbling at tree bark), make sure the cage or guard is large enough for expansion and can be easily removed once the tree grows.

When ornamental trees are planted, they should be staked.

Landscapers tell you trees do not really like to be staked. Staking originated when most trees were planted bareroot. Occasionally a tree in a very windy spot will need a single stake on the prevailing wind side. Often, the tree ends up holding up the broken stake. Worse, if the stakes are not eventually removed, the wires left on the tree will girdle and kill it.

You can tap only the sugar maple to get good sap.

First, keep in mind that all maples (not just the sugar maple) have sweet, edible sap and can be tapped. Some people recall tapping sycamores, birches, walnuts, and hickories, something the early settlers and Native Americans did. Do saps vary in flavor? Indeed. Sycamore sap has a lower sugar concentration and the finished product is inferior to maple. Hickories and walnuts produce a sweet sap whose products are inferior to maple sap, some believe. Black walnut and butternut make distinctive syrups. Nut trees can be tapped in

the same way maples are, and no matter which tree is tapped, it's a lot of hard work.

It takes 30 to 40 or even 50 gallons of sap to produce a gallon of syrup. Norway maple and sugar maple are good producers. In fact, most maples are producers of sap with high sugar content. Black and yellow birch are good producers, although it takes more sap per gallon of syrup.

When you buy a fruit tree, select the oldest and largest caliper tree.

You can get in a real debate over the size of bare-root fruit-tree stock. You can buy 1-year-old and 2-year-old trees, but we don't think they should be any older, because older trees do not take hold as quickly as younger trees. Younger trees come into bearing sooner after planting than older ones. Nothing is gained by planting "bearing age" fruit trees. A healthy 1-year whip is preferable to an older tree that has been stunted by spending too much time in a nursery. Remember, the digging process destroys almost 98 percent of the roots and a young tree can stand this abuse better than older stock.

Trees dug with wire baskets should have the wire cut after planting.

You can get in an argument over this one. We've checked with dozens of landscapers who do not cut the wire baskets after planting. Manufacturers tell us that the wire corrodes eventually and does not seriously interfere with tree roots.

Note: If your tree's root ball is wrapped in a synthetic burlap, it is plastic, does not biodegrade, and must be removed.

Tall trees should never have the top cut out. It ruins the shape, according to arborists.

There are times when judicial pruning is necessary and if not done, trees will grow out of bound. Homeowners often have a tall tree that needs "topping" — that is, the top should be cut out. To some arborists, "topping" is a dirty word. Topping is just another word for "pollarding" — an ancient practice of cutting out the top. In medieval times, trees were "topped" — pollarded for fuel. Today, Europeans pollard for spatial reasons. Some think that pollarding reduces tree life. Others say no. As long as the public continues to plant trees that grow too tall for their site, topping will be necessary. If done correctly, cutting the top out of a tree is a safe and sensible practice that does not ruin the shape of the tree or shorten its life.

A large tree should be cut down if it has a few dead limbs on it.

We've seen a lot of good trees cut down for firewood because they had a few rotten limbs. A few dead limbs don't mean the tree is dying. A tree limb is like a human tooth — it should be saved if possible. Get an expert to evaluate the situation. Cut out the dead limbs. Even in a wood lot, we think some dead trees should be left for birds. Some birds need dead trees for their survival.

We should make an effort to save all the trees we can, because in America they are dying at the rate of 1,000,000 a year. One study reports that a tree with a trunk 2 inches (5 cm) in diameter has a cooling ability equal to a $150 air conditioner using 40¢ per day in electricity. A tree 7 inches (18 cm) in diameter equals an $850 air conditioner using $5 per day.

You should never plant trees, shrubs, or flowers in summer because they'll burn up.

False. Early spring and fall have been the traditional times for planting, but with the development of many methods of growing plants and modern transplanting equipment, planting at other times of the year has become possible and may be quite desirable. Plants that are balled and burlapped may be planted at any time they are available. Container-grown plants are also candidates for planting at any time, but regular watering is essential. Bare-root stock is best handled and planted during the dormant season.

If you dump rusty nails around a florist hydrangea plant it will bloom.

Iron has nothing to do with blooming. Try moving the plant closer to the house for protection, or dig it up and bring it indoors for the winter. Hydrangeas have both flower buds

and leaf buds. Flower buds are not hardy and will winterkill
when the temperature drops. Leaf buds are hardy and will
not winterkill. Hydrangea plants often produce lots of
leaves but no flowers because the cold temperatures ruin the
flower buds.

**Some evergreens can be planted and left alone, needing
no care.**

There's no such thing. All evergreens need some care.
Evergreens like an organic mulch, such as sawdust, bark, or
wood chips. In windy locations they need winter protection,
especially on the side facing winds. This can be burlap
wraps (never use plastic) or an "anti-transpiration" spray,
applied in late fall.

   Never let evergreens go into the winter with a dry soil,
especially those planted recently. In a foundation planting,
evergreens need a few minutes of shearing each year to keep
them within bounds. Do not wait until they grow into a jungle
and then butcher them. They'll look sorry, like a plucked
chicken. Evergreens are not heavy feeders, so go easy on
plant foods. They'll get their sustenance from the organic
mulch.

Acid-loving plants such as azaleas and rhododendrons like acid rain better than non–acid-loving plants.

The so-called acid-lovers (azaleas, rhododendrons, and so on) really don't like the acid. The problem is that if the soil is not acidic enough, nutrients such as iron are tied up and plants cannot absorb them. In an acidic soil, the iron, magnesium, and other nutrients are "unlocked" and can be taken up by the plant, giving the foliage a healthy green color. If the iron is tied-up in a sweet (alkaline or nonacidic) soil, leaves become yellowed or chlorotic. So, in an acidic soil, iron becomes free for the plant to use.

Acid-loving plants would benefit from acid rain *if* the amount of acid could be controlled and if it could reach the soil without hitting the leaves. Throughout the world acid rain is becoming more of a problem because concentrations are detrimentally high.

7.
Lawns and
Ground
Covers

When operating a lawnmower, it's easier to pull it than to push it.

False. When operating a mower, push rather than pull it. Pushing enables the operator to see exactly where the mower is going. Each year many operators suffer serious injury by pulling a mower backward to the danger point — where the housing hits the front of their feet. Once the housing is pulled back over the foot, an accident is imminent!

Zoysia is a perfect lawn grass. It's been around for 800 years and withstands droughts, floods, pestilence, and traffic.

Zoysia is tough and it does what is claimed, but you should think twice about planting it. It's not a perfect grass. The worst feature is that the grass loses its color early in fall. It's straw-colored in fall and winter, accounting for zoysia's lack of popularity. Another factor: It's very aggressive and can creep into your vegetable garden, becoming difficult to eradicate.

The best person to ask is the one who has grown it firsthand. We have grown it and do not recommend it as a substitute for other grasses. What is needed is more research on it, because some day it may meet the demands of our changing environment.

Lawns that have that gray look need more fertilizer.

False. One reason lawns have a gray-yellow look after mowing is because of a dull blade. When a steel blade whirls at 200 miles per hour against leaves of grass, its sharpness determines the health and appearance of a lawn. A dull blade can result in a gray-brown, frazzled lawn, regardless of what kind of grass is present. A dull mower blade tears grass tips, leaving shreds that turn color quickly. The unsightly, frayed edges also can provide an entry for disease organisms.

To prevent this, sharpen blades regularly. During spring, grass grows lush and soft and does not dull the blades quickly. However, as summer progresses, grass turns tough and wiry, dulling the blades faster. Even your ear can tell if a blade is sharp. When it cuts, it makes a neat hissing sound.

There is a chemical you can spray on grass to keep it short, eliminating the need for mowing.

There have been growth regulators for turf, but for the home gardener or homeowner, we doubt if they are so good that you can say goodbye to your lawnmower. The Lawn Institute says these chemicals need very careful application and may cause undesirable side effects. They must be sprayed on evenly; a slight under- or overdose can mean waste or damage. Also, all grass varieties and lawn weeds do not respond alike to a growth suppressant, so you may get an uneven appearance.

We question the use of chemical mowing. Lawn experts are also questioning the use of chemicals for disease control. They say that modern grasses are bred for tolerance to disease. With proper care, disease symptoms will be mild, with no one fungus getting out of hand.

Putting in artificial grass or blacktop saves maintenance time and prevents pollution.

False move. Artificial grass heats up under a hot sun, sending midday air temperatures way up. Blacktop is even worse for holding heat. Artificial turf is not cheap, either. Stick with live grass, even if it's half weeds.

All green plants give us oxygen, cool the air, and clean the atmosphere. Neither humans nor other animals could exist without plants.

To make a wildflower garden, just sow the seed, water it, and watch it grow. It will be easier to maintain than a lawn.

It would be nice if you could sow wildflower seed, and then sit back and reap the colorful benefits with no further attention paid to the newly created environment. Wildflower gardens aren't as easy to grow as many gardeners think. Some wildflowers, such as yarrow, are too easy to grow and they take over.

Wildflowers can add color and natural beauty, but the spot can become an eyesore if it gets overrun with weeds. You don't spread wildflower seeds on a lawn and expect them to grow. You will need to till the soil to a depth of 8 inches, then remove the weeds and rake smooth. Tilling brings up weeds (an acre of soil has about 3,000 pounds of weed seeds). Watch out for mixes containing annual rye grass or timothy, as these spread and crowd out wildflowers. In addition to this, some weed and grass seeds live in the soil for 1,700 years or so and will germinate to compete with your wildflower planting.

One way to keep weeds down before planting is to let the plowed area remain fallow (unworked) for a month or so, pulling any weeds that sprout. Some people use a weedkiller to kill both weeds and seeds. If you do this, don't sow seed for at least 6 months. Fertilizer is not needed, as it encourages weed growth.

The meadow will have to be mowed annually to keep it in a permanent state of early succession. Here are some plants you might find in a typical wildflower mixture: coreopsis, purple coneflower *(Echinacea)*, black-eyed Susan *(Rudbeckia)*, Indian blanket *(Gaillardia)*, Shirley poppy, and delphinium or rocket larkspur. Check with your County Extension Service about putting in a wildflower lawn because there may be a local ordinance against it.

Letting the grass grow taller saves grass strength. Regular clipping ruins the grass by sapping its strength.

Lawn-mowing is a necessary practice for the development of a tight turf cover. It encourages individual grass plants to thicken and provides a good, uniform appearance.

A good rule of thumb for mowing home lawns is not to remove any more than one-third of the grass blade surface at any one time. If this rule is followed, you no longer need to bag your grass clippings. Leave clippings on the lawn for their fertility value. The only exception is when the grass is allowed to grow 6 inches or so before you cut it. When this happens, remove the clippings or they may cause disease problems.

Lawns have a high water requirement.

The American Lawn Institute states that most lawns do not have high water requirements. Those located in areas of limited rainfall will often go dormant if there is a shortage of rainfall. Lawns situated in cool, humid regions of the country need about an inch of water a week, or about 12 inches over the summer, to stay green.

A lawn that's watered regularly is healthier than one that isn't.

Americans have a tendency to overwater lawns. Grass specialists will tell you that an occasional drying out can be therapeutic and will often prevent diseases and weed sprouting. Drying out tends to drive the roots deeper, whereas constant watering can cause shallow rooting (which in turn makes grass more susceptible to drought).

A lawn should be mown two or three times a week.

There is no point in mowing three times per week. It could harm the lawn rather than help it. When you mow a lawn you are "harvesting" the grass, and when you remove the clippings you are removing the nutrients contained in the grass from the lawn. For example, 100 pounds (44.8 kg) of fresh grass from the lawn contains 11 ounces (.32 kg) of nitrogen, 1.6 ounces (.045 kg) of phosphorus, and 8 ounces (.23 kg) of potassium. To put it another way, clippings on one acre of lawn have about 40 pounds (18 kg) of nitrogen in a season.

Potassium in the grass clippings is available almost immediately, whereas the nitrogen and phosphorus become available over a period of weeks as the clippings decompose. That's good. Grass clippings are the original, slow-release fertilizer. It's a sin to bag them and put them on the curb for the landfill. They make a wonderful mulch and nitrogen source for the compost pile.

High-powered pesticides and fertilizers are essential ingredients for lush lawns.

You can have a healthy garden and yard without them, despite the fact that suburban homeowners and commercial landscapers are spraying more pesticides and fertilizers per acre than U.S. farmers apply to cropland. Busy or part-time gardeners have many alternatives to chemicals: Fight weeds by hand pulling or using a mulch, both old-fashioned and effective alternatives. Recycling grass clippings and leaves as mulch not only keeps weeds down and saves moisture but also improves the soil (either heavy or light). For bugs, insecticidal soaps (Safer's brand, for example) or diatomaceous earth (made up of remains of one-celled plants that lived in the sea some 30 million years ago) can be a defense against slugs and other soft-bodied insects.

Also, many beneficial insects such as lacewings, tachinid flies, trichogramma wasps, and various strains of bacteria fight gypsy moths, mosquitoes, and Colorado potato beetles. New pheromone traps use synthetic sex hormones to lure pests to an orgiastic death. We let birds eat the grubs in our lawn.

The more you feed your lawn, the thicker it gets.

Feeding is good up to a point, but not all fertilization is beneficial. A heavy dose of nitrogen will encourage a lot of leaf growth, but it can also repress root growth, leading to thatch buildup and poor drought tolerance. Some of the worst lawns we've seen are those that have had heavy doses of fertilizer. A modest amount over a longer time is much better than heavy doses applied frequently.

If you get moss on your lawn, it will crowd out the grass.

Moss does not crowd out grass. It moves in where there is no grass. Moss growth normally starts with fall rains and peaks in early spring. Since most grasses grow poorly (if at all) in winter, mosses invade and dominate lawns in only a few months. Moss declines in summer as conditions become drier and turfgrass growth increases. In shade, in poorly drained soil, or under irrigation, moss grows throughout the summer and can tolerate long periods of drought in a dehydrated condition. It will "rehydrate" and grow with the onset of fall rains.

Moss invasion causes thin turf.

Thin turf may be due to low fertility, highly acidic soils, too much shade, insects, or disease. Use a good lawn fertilizer and reseed in fall.

Feeding and mowing your lawn causes pollution of the water and air.

In an age of environmental concern, many people fear that feeding lawns will pollute ground water. Unless slow-release fertilizers are used, the fertilizer applied to lawns is often carried off by heavy rains into surface water. Excess fertilizer can easily pollute surface water (though not ground water, generally).

The key to curing moss problems is to apply lime.

Liming alone does not cure moss problems. Too much shade, poor drainage, and lack of fertility are causes of moss. Liming a soil can raise the pH to between 6 and 6.5, making the soil less acidic and thus less hospitable to moss, but it is not a guaranteed cure.

Feed your lawn in fall. Also, thin out trees to let light in. When planting new lawns in shady sites, be sure to use shade-tolerant species. In dry shade, use fine fescues. In wet, shady spots, roughstalk bluegrass persists better than other grasses.

Spring is the best time to seed a lawn.

Nature's way is usually the best way after all. And seeding in autumn, rather than spring, comes close to being nature's way. By this time of year, temperatures are cooling off, days are getting shorter, and soil moisture is ideal for germination of seed and early seedling establishment. Also, at this time many annual weeds, such as crabgrass, have finished their growth cycle and will not compete with seedling lawngrass plants.

The value of turfgrass has been vastly overrated by grass-seed people.

Turfgrass acts as a very efficient filter for pollutants in air and water. Grass blades take in carbon dioxide (waste) and the worst atmospheric pollutants and give back pure oxygen. Grass modifies temperature. Turfgrass is the safest playing surface for athletes, stands up well to foot traffic, and protects the soil from wind and water erosion. It enhances real estate values and relates to community beautification. Don't hesitate to spend time and money on a lawn. People see it more than they do such things as drapes and furniture.

If you mow your lawn very short, you'll have to mow it less often.

No. People think that if you mow a lawn short, you have to mow it less, but that's a fallacy. We'll try to explain why grass grows faster if you cut it short. When clipped short, the grass must replace its ability to make food fast, or die out. It's a battle for survival. With a higher clipping height, there is more leaf surface (the food maker) and there is less need to make food, since the life of the grass is not threatened (it's in better shape than shortly clipped grass). In other words, when grass is clipped short, every ounce of energy left in the plant goes to replace the lost leaf surface or the plant will die without leaves to make food.

Putting greens on golf courses are cut every day because at ¼ inch (6 mm) or less, the grass is so badly defoliated that the plants are always about to starve to death. At lawn heights of 1½ to 3 inches (38–57 mm) you get ½ to 1 inch (6–12 mm) of growth in about 7 days. Let the clippings filter back to the soil. Do not bag and cart them away. In short, close clipping does not mean you mow a lawn less often, but more often. Nature says to a close-clipped lawn, get growing or you'll die out!

Rotary blades use a suction effect to stand the grass up straight and then rip the tip of the plant in a scythe-like manner. Reel blades use a cleaner, more efficient scissors-like action with the blade slicing off the turfgrass. In cool, wet periods you should use a higher cut to promote deep rooting.

Leaving clippings on the lawn will contribute to thatch buildup.

False! In a nutshell, thatch is a layer of dead plant tissue on the soil surface. When it builds up it can act like a thatched roof and shed water away from roots. It consists of dead grass leaves and grass roots, underground creeping stems that are high in lignin, a cell wall material that does not break down easily. Grass clippings do *not* contribute to thatch, as they contain only a tiny amount of lignin.

People catch grass clippings because they think it causes thatch. They don't like the looks of drying clippings left by traditional mowers, and they hate to track them into the house.

More and more homeowners are changing their mowing habits. They belong to a group called "Don't Bag It" and they mow more often — maybe five times a month, instead of four. Although you will mow more often, you will find the job takes 40 percent less time because there is no bag to bother with. When the lawn grows slowly, you can mow less often. A good rule of thumb is to never cut more than one-third of the lawn height.

Most rotary mowers do a pretty good job of chopping the clippings and blowing them out. The new mulching mowers work even better, as they grind the grass blades into small pieces that drop to the ground and disappear quickly. If you have an older mower, don't worry because the clippings from an ordinary mower do get cut up in fine pieces and will break down readily. Grass clippings are too valuable to throw away.

Lawnmowers pollute the air. People should get rid of gasoline lawnmowers and buy a push type for a cleaner atmosphere.

If you have a postage-stamp–sized lawn, a hand-powered push mower makes sense because of better exercise and less pollution. Push mowers are making a comeback. We're all polluters — we breathe. If you don't mow your lawn, it will turn into a jungle and devalue your home. If you are worried about your gas mower creating pollution, consider replacing it with an electric mower. Some models have rechargeable batteries, eliminating the cumbersome cord.

Fairy rings in a lawn are due to the soil being too acidic. Adding lime will cure it.

Mushrooms (toadstools) often grow in a circular arrangement on lawns; these are called "fairy rings." Rings can be anywhere from 3 to 9 inches (8–23 cm) wide and can encircle an area from a few inches to 30 feet (7 cm–9 m) in diameter. For centuries, people believed these fairy rings were from elves, leprechauns, and fairies dancing at night. The rings reappear in the same spot year after year, but each summer the diameter will be larger than it was the year before.

If you observe the rings for a few weeks, here is what you will notice:

1. A dark green ring appears in the grass.
2. A week or two later, the fungal fruiting bodies (mushrooms) appear.
3. The grass in the rings stops growing and turns yellow.

The grass in the ring is lush and green at first, due to rain and microorganisms that secrete enzymes, releasing nitrogen. This is like feeding the grass a nitrogen fertilizer. Shortly after the mushrooms fade and die, the grass in the ring turns yellow-green due to a shortage of nutrients. Thus, the grass in the ring has gone from feast to famine.

There is no way to control fairy rings. You find them in areas where a tree was cut down. The rotting roots make a good food for the mushroom. Some people dig them up and haul in fresh soil. Too difficult! Pick off the mushrooms as you see them and discard. The best advice is to live with fairy rings and look at them as one of nature's interesting works of art. Don't spend money on chemicals to fight them. Toadstools are nature's way of breaking down organic matter. Adding lime is useless!

We want to plant a ground cover in a problem area. We want something that doesn't need mowing, grows in poor soil, and grows fast, yet doesn't get out of bounds, takes sun or shade, tolerates drought and wet spots, and doesn't attract snakes.

There's no such ground cover. There are ground covers that will grow in certain trouble spots, but not one that will do well in all. In short, ground covers are not the answer to the lazy gardener who wants to set out plants, wave a magic wand, and watch the plants grow. The best ground cover you can get (if you have the right conditions) is plain grass. But if you have deep shade, steep banks, or awkward corners, then the right selection of ground cover plants will work better than grass.

I want to start a wildflower collection. Digging plants from the wild is the cheapest and easiest way.

False. Most wildflowers dug from the wild simply die. In many areas this is illegal to do. It also further depletes already dwindling populations of many species. Buy your plants from a reputable nursery selling only commercially propagated, not wild-collected, plants.

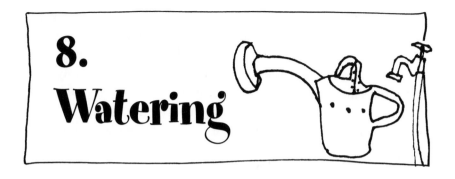

8. Watering

Acid rain is just environmental propaganda.

False. Every time it rains, it's not pennies from heaven but
corrosive acid that's showering down on the earth. Rainwater,
especially in the eastern United States, has become increas-
ingly acidic in the past 15 or 20 years. Data from New York
and New England show that rainwater is one-third dilute
nitric acid and two-thirds dilute sulfuric acid. The acidity at
its worst is equivalent to vinegar or lemon juice. The average
pH (acidity) in upstate New York is 4. Freshwater bodies
where the problem is acute are endangered by acid rainfall.

Gardeners can still use rainwater if they collect it in a
barrel. Test the soil periodically, and neutralize the acidity
by adding the recommended amount of limestone.

**Chlorinated tap water causes damage to houseplants, so it
is a good idea to collect rainwater for houseplants.**

Not necessarily. Household bleach is added to tap water
until it's identical with drinking water injected with chlorine

gas, and it doesn't seem to harm most plants, except African violets. High concentrations of chlorine will damage geraniums, petunias, marigolds, and kalanchoe — we're sure of this. Fortunately it's easy to avoid chlorine burn. Simply draw off a pail of water at night and let it sit until the next day. By then, the chlorine gas will have dissipated.

Fluoride is something different. It will cause tip burn and leaf scorch on all members of the lily family. *Dracaenas,* spider plants *(Chlorophytum),* lilies, and others are sensitive to fluoride injury. Water treated with fluoride differs from that treated with chlorine in that the fluoride will not evaporate. It remains in the water. However, it's a simple matter to prevent fluoride injury: Add a tablespoon (15 ml) of ground limestone to a potted plant before you water it. The calcium in the limestone locks up the fluoride, making it unavailable to plants.

Well water that contains large amounts of calcium and iron is harmful to young trees and plants.

Don't hesitate to use the water on plants because some nutrients will be added. It is possible that too much hard water (calcium) can be harmful to acid-loving plants such as azaleas, rhododendrons, gardenias, pin oaks, and others. If the leaves start to get yellow or mottled due to the calcium, you can use aluminum sulfate (1 teaspoon per square foot, or 5 ml per 0.3 m).

For indoor use, the situation is different. Try one of the following: (1) Water houseplants with the water collected in a dehumidifier (which is distilled water); (2) every few months, use a fertilizer designed for acid-loving plants (e.g., Miracid) to counteract the calcium; or (3) collect rainwater in barrels.

You shouldn't use old aquarium water for houseplants and shrubs.

There's no reason why you can't. In fact, many people water their houseplants with aquarium water, with no ill effects.

The water is rich in nitrogen and benefits all plants. However, we would hesitate to use it on edible crops until more research is done.

We have a water softener and were told not to use softened water on houseplants because it would kill them.

Not necessarily. In many cases, water passing through a softener does have a harmful effect on plants. Softeners exchange the calcium (harmless) for sodium (harmful). Sodium is harmful because it tends to make the soil sticky, and sodium soil can also be toxic to plants that are sensitive. If you have a softener, don't worry too much because there's a simple trick to eliminate the sodium hazard. Since the softener takes calcium out, why not add it back to the water to restore that which was present before softening removed it? This simply nullifies the effect of the sodium added in the softening process.

Here's all you do: Go to your garden center or farm store and buy some gypsum (calcium sulfate), a very cheap and harmless form of calcium. It has low solubility yet can be dissolved to treat softened water. One-half level teaspoon added to a gallon of softened water or 1 tablespoon per 6 gallons of water is enough to supply the necessary calcium to change the softened water back to the "unsoftened" water. We hope this simple trick will settle the controversy over water softeners. You can draw enough water off for your houseplants and add gypsum to it, thus eliminating any risks involving plants.

Note: Many home gardeners use gypsum on their gardens to help loosen up a clay soil. The cost is small, and gypsum is a harmless source of calcium.

Note also: Hard water may be bad for the house plumbing and laundry, but it's good for your body's pipes, according to a scientist at Oak Ridge National Laboratory. In tests involving 505 farmers, it was found that calcium in hard water meant less risk of heart disease. Calcium and magnesium also lower the body's intake of cadmium and lead, two harmful substances.

Every summer our well gets low and we are in danger of running out of water for the garden. Can we use dishwater and bath water for vegetables, berries, and fruit trees? I heard that soap would kill the plants.

It's a good idea to use dishwater and bath water on your vegetables, grapes, roses, raspberries, and so on. The dishwater may contain washing liquids, or powdered soap, but these are seldom harmful if applied to the soil near the plants. It's a good idea to use tap water from time to time to "dilute" or flush out any compound that might be building up. By all means, save and use your bath water if you can.

A drought has one good effect: It teaches people to recycle water. One reader wrote to us: "I hooked up a drain hose to my washing machine to save the rinse water. It worked just fine on ageratums, wax begonias, lobelias, marigolds, gladiolus, and assorted shrubs, even my tomatoes,

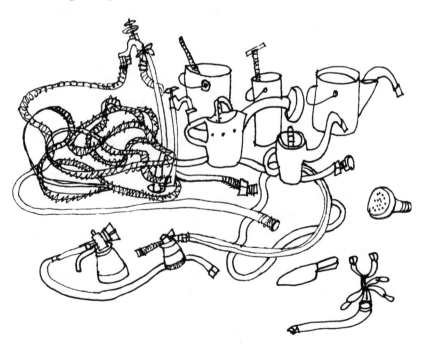

and with *no bad effects.* Another great source is window air conditioners. We've placed buckets under their drains and use this water, too."

Dozens of people have written to tell us that dishwater (with liquid detergents) is perfectly safe for porch pots, window boxes, gardens, trees, shrubs, and so on. The detergent you use in your washing machine or dishwasher contains sodium and sometimes bleach, so you should dilute any water you save with plain tap water, since sodium is apt to make the soil sticky and bleach is harmful to plants and soil organisms.

My sister lives on a farm and she has limited house water. She saves all her dishwashing water and pours it on her indoor and outdoor plants. Her impatiens and others are the most beautiful we've ever seen, and she uses dishwashing water only. She uses no fertilizers and attributes all her success to nutrients in the spent water.

How about bath water? It's also safe to use on houseplants, but it's awkward to collect it. What about phosphates? No need to worry. Phosphates have been banned in dishwashing detergents.

A moisture meter is important for growing better plants.

Your thumb and forefinger make a good moisture meter: Touch the upper surface of the soil to see if it is moist or not.

Some people have luck with moisture meters. They work by electrolytic action, measuring the conductivity of the minerals in the soil, rather than the soil moisture itself. But they can be misleading. You could get a "wet" reading in a soil that is bone-dry but high in salts from fertilizers, and a "dry" reading if the soil is neutral and you had just watered with purified water. An inventor by the name of John Voloudakis has come up with a patented probe that gathers a soil sample at different levels of the pot — it's called "Terraprobe," a rod inserted into the soil. Give it a turn, pull it up, and you get soil samples at four different depths.

Two reliable indicators of soil moisture content are touch and weight. Feel the soil with your fingers and lift the pot. A watered pot is heavier than a dry one. Also, tapping a clay pot with a metal pipe gives some indication of moisture content: A "ring" means the pot is dry, a thud means the pot is watered enough.

A lollipop stick is also a good moisture indicator. Insert a dry stick into the soil. Pull it out. If soil particles cling to it, the plant has enough moisture. If it comes out with no particles, the soil is too dry.

9.

Soil

You can tell if a soil is good by its smell and feel.

Farmers and gardeners can judge soil by its smell. Responsible for the rich earthy odor are two gases: geosmin and 2-methylisoborneol, produced by fungi and actinomycetes ("act-tin-oh-my-seats") — rod-shaped bacteria found in soil. You can thank the soil microbes for this delightful aroma. The more of these microbes in the soil, the more organically active and healthy it is. Microbiologists found that virgin woodland soil produced over 20 times the gases that cropland did. Just a teaspoon of soil from your garden contains billions of various organisms that make your soil a living jungle, so in good soil you can actually smell the byproduct (gas) of these microbes.

Black soil is better than mineral soils or "peat-lite" mixes.

Soil color has little to do with quality. Black soils are higher in organic matter than lighter soils, but they may be low in certain nutrients.

For plants to thrive, the soil should provide good air and water drainage around the roots. Muck dug from swamps or bogs is not suitable for potting soil or starting seeds.

Our garden soil is full of clay. We've been told to give up on gardening because clay is tough to work.

Don't feel all that hopeless! Heavy clay soils can be tamed to produce good crops. Let's understand what a clay soil is. The clay particles are so fine that they are less than 1/12,000 of an inch. In other words, 12,000 particles side-by-side span an inch. Because they are so small, they can pack together very tightly, making it difficult for roots to move through them. Because they are so tight, they also tend not to allow easy movement of the oxygen needed by roots, particularly during wet periods or if they are overwatered. Trees in heavy clay soils do not develop a deep root system and can be easily toppled by strong winds. Clay particles are not all bad, however; they do much to hold and exchange nutrients in soil.

Adding sand to a soil full of clay will loosen it up and improve drainage.

False! Sand can make clay soil even worse. Drainage of a soil depends on soil pore space. Coarse sand has 40 percent large pore space and will drain very well. Clay has very small pore space and that's why it drains poorly. If you mix sand with clay, the clay particles reduce the number of pore spaces, making the drainage worse, not better.

What's the best way to loosen up a tight, clay soil? Organic matter in any form — peat moss, rotted manure, leaves, sawdust, compost — anything organic works. Another thing you can do is add gypsum. Gypsum has the ability to make fine clay particles lump together, creating larger particles and therefore more pore space.

Sand and perlite, both added to a potting soil, help improve drainage, especially if peat moss is in the mixture.

Potting soils bought in stores are better than homemade types.

Not necessarily. Some store soils are pure muck, very bad for houseplants and starting seeds. Many of them are "fluffed up" until they are as fine as flour. Their fibrous structure has been broken down and that is why we recommend adding perlite, at least one third by volume.

Some potting mixes contain high-salt fertilizers. Furthermore, when the mixes are stored in bags, they are apt to heat up due to the activity of microorganisms, which results in salt production. Thus you get two "shots" of salts.

There are as many "recipes" for soil mixes as there are gardeners. Whatever you do, don't use any garden soil in the mixture for starting seeds unless you sterilize it first. It's okay to use some in a mix for growing houseplants, however. A mix of equal parts sand, peat moss, garden loam, and perlite (or vermiculite) makes a good houseplant potting soil. We mention this one because a good many old-timers still want to use a bit of garden soil to give "backbone" to the mix.

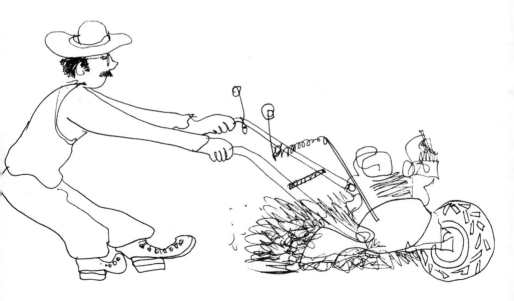

You can sterilize garden soil by placing it in a turkey roasting bag and baking it at 250°F (122°C) for about half an hour. Sterilized soil won't harm seedlings.

Gardeners who are doing indoor light gardening recommend several recipes for potting soil. The Indoor Gardening Society of America recommends two or three mixes. Here's one: one part sphagnum peat moss, one part vermiculite, one part perlite, one tablespoon (15 ml) ground limestone or dolomitic lime for every 7 quarts (7 liters) or ½ to 1 cup (140–280 ml) of crushed eggshells per quart (liter) of mix. This mixture is good for almost any houseplant.

Note: Eggshells make a good ingredient in potting soil. Wash them and when you have enough, whirl them in the blender or crush them with a rolling pin. Or you can soak them in water and use the liquid for houseplants.

It's a good idea to add clean kitty litter to potting soil.

It is *not* good business to add cat litter to your soil, especially one containing odor-masking ingredients. A good potting soil contains the right ingredients *without* adding kitty litter. Cat litter may lighten a soil, but it's too expensive. Sand or perlite would work better. Never use spent cat litter in potting soil or around edible crops such as onions or radishes because of the possibility of spreading certain diseases.

Our flowers and vegetable crops are always poor. We have been told that it's because the soil is acidic and needs lime.

Not necessarily. When plants exhibit poor growth in the garden, the first thing that pops into some minds is soil acidity, expressed by the symbol "pH." This two-letter term is the measure of acidity or alkalinity — in this case, of soil. The pH scale ranges from 1 to 14 — the lower numbers represent acid conditions, whereas the higher numbers indicate alkaline conditions. A pH of 7 indicates a neutral soil, that is, neither acid nor alkaline. Most crops prefer a slightly acidic soil. The grass in your lawn likes a fairly wide pH range, from 5.5 to 7.5, with the best growth in a range of around 6.5, which is slightly acidic.

Lime is used to make acidic soils more alkaline, and sulfur or iron sulfate is used to make alkaline soils more acidic. The lime used in lawns and gardens is ground limestone containing calcium carbonate. Since its action in changing acidity is slow, fall is an excellent time to apply lime. But keep in mind that too much lime causes more harm than good.

Poor growth can be due to many factors other than soil acidity. Disease, grubs, overfeeding, overwatering, weather, and other problems all affect plant growth.

Note: Wood ashes are a good substitute for lime and can be used in the garden or on the lawn.

We had a poor garden last year. Someone said we should have our soil analyzed.

Not necessarily. Some people think that testing your soil will enable you to turn your "dirt" into horticultural gold. Some myth!

Remember, your soil is a living universe, loaded with all kinds of living things, a galaxy of microbes. Any soil loaded with organic matter is bound to produce fruits, flowers, and vegetables. Soil test kits can be a lot of fun for anyone who likes to fill test tubes, stir solutions, and watch liquids change color. The kits tend to reduce the idea of fertility to the levels of nitrogen, phosphorus, and potassium (NPK), or they measure the pH (acidity level) of the soil. Both of these tests ignore the organic content, the backbone of any healthy garden. One of the problems with soil analysis is the difficulty in interpreting the results. Any balanced fertilizer added to a soil containing organic matter is enough to give you a soil that supports most plant growth.

In most cases, a nutrient shortage is not the main cause of poor gardens. Often it's poor drainage, shade, or some cultural practice such as overwatering or not enough watering. A so-called soil analysis tells you nothing about insects or diseases lurking in the earth. Soil tests might be the only way to determine specific deficiencies. But a soil test is just one tool — it alone won't solve all your gardening problems. A good soil involves more than the big three plant nutrients and the soil pH.

My husband is a fanatic about removing rocks and stones from his garden. He is constantly picking them up and carting them away. Does it do any good to remove them? Where do they come from?

I had an aunt who was the same way. She picked so many stones she had to "use a ladder" to get down into her garden. Some garden soils seem perpetually filled with rocks and stones, and the more you pick them up, the more they come to the surface. We went to an engineer to get the answer.

There is a phenomenon called "upfreezing," which causes a brand-new crop of rocks to surface every year, no matter how many you have laboriously removed the previous year. Geologists tell us this is due to the fact that water expands as it freezes, but they aren't sure what causes the rocks to rise in the soil. There are two theories: (1) Frost-push: During a freeze, cold penetrates downward, through the rocks more rapidly than through the surrounding soil. So any water beneath a rock freezes first, nudging the rock upward. During a thaw, a "pedestal" of ice keeps the rock in place long enough for the soil around it to drop into the cavity left behind when it rose; (2) Frost-pull: During a cold snap, soil freezes first around the top of the rock, gripping it tightly. As this soil expands upward (call it frost-heave) it pulls the rock with it, and loose soil slumps into the vacated cavity. So much for the great stone debate.

Does it do any good to remove the stones and rocks from the garden? Some doubt it when you think how big the earth is, and what a pile of stones remains underneath. It could go on forever! But it's helpful to remove big rocks, especially if you use a power tiller.

10.
Compost, Mulch, and Fertilizers

Compost piles smell, attract rodents, and take a lot of work.

False. If a compost smells, you're doing something wrong. The only necessary equipment for composting is a rake or fork to turn the pile over once or twice. Bins aren't needed to hold a compost pile. They may need to be watered once or twice in dry weather, but there's no need for fertilizer, lime, fancy bins, or scientifically measured layers.

Do not add meat, grease, bones, or dairy products to a compost pile. It could make the material smell and attract flies, rodents, and other pests.

If you live in an urban or suburban area and want to compost kitchen waste, but have little room and don't want to encourage insects and animals, try "garbage can composting":

1. Use a galvanized (or plastic) garbage can with a lid that fits well, and punch several small holes in the bottom.
2. Add 3 inches of good soil to the can.
3. Add some "angleworms" or "red worms" (sometimes referred to as manure worms or red wrigglers). *Note:* worms are optional, but it takes longer to break down the compost without them.
4. Set the can on two cement blocks with something beneath to catch any liquid draining out. This liquid is usually odorless and can be used on houseplants, potted plants, or garden plants.
5. Throw in kitchen wastes — potato peelings, lettuce leaves, coffee grounds, tea leaves — that ordinarily go into the garbage can.
6. Each addition of fresh garbage may be covered with a sprinkling of soil or shredded leaves, newspapers (best if ripped into long strips), grass clippings, sawdust, and so on.
7. To fortify the mixture, sprinkle on a little liquid plant food from time to time.

Odor is usually lacking, but coffee grounds can be added as a natural deodorant. If any odor should develop, shredded newspapers will take care of it almost immediately. Eggshells add calcium; and even if they don't break down immediately, they will return into the soil as filler.

Avoid onions and onion skins. Worms don't like them. However, worms do tolerate citrus skins in moderate amounts.

One regular-size garbage can composter will take care of a family of two adults and two children. Some families start one garbage can in the fall, add another if this one fills up before spring, then dump and start over again. Others have two cans at the same time. A garage is a good place to keep the can. If your can contains worms, it must be stored in an area with above-freezing temperatures.

Walnut leaves and walnuts themselves are not a suitable material to use in a compost pile. They will cause the composted material to give off the same sort of walnut poisoning that the walnut roots give off.

When leaves and walnut husks are added to the compost pile, juglone is diluted and broken down by microorganisms (see p. 47). When the composted material is spread on the garden, it's so diluted as to be harmless. Thus you have little to worry about when the walnut parts are composted.

Bonemeal makes a good bulb fertilizer.

False. Back in the old days, bonemeal was used for bulbs and all kinds of flowers and vegetables, and it did a good job. Today, bonemeal isn't what it used to be. Three decades ago bonemeal was made from bones, cartilage, and other tissue scraps. At that time it was a good source of nitrogen, phosphorus, and many micronutrients. Not so today. It consists only of bones that have had their nitrogen-rich marrow steamed out to make gelatin by-products. Much of the nitrogen and most of the micronutrients are gone, although the phosphorus content is there. Perhaps bonemeal is okay if worked down into the root zone and not used as top dressing, since the phosphorus is mostly insoluble and will not work down in. Plants need nitrogen, phosphorus, and potash, so why not use a balanced fertilizer containing all three? Any garden center sells balanced plant foods.

We have lots of newspapers and want to use them for a mulch in the garden. Some say the ink on them is toxic to plants.

These days some newspaper ink is made of soybeans and is harmless in the garden. In fact, Penn State has developed a mulch made from newspapers, magazines, and other paper. The new product is called "Pennmulch." It consists of small

green pellets that resemble rabbit food. The mulch can be spread by hand and can be used in vegetable gardens as well as around ornamental plantings.

After all you say about using a mulch around trees and shrubs, I just read a report that mulching does *not* save water, but actually increases water loss.

We read the report you mention and couldn't believe what we read. Studies at Texas A&M compared water use on shrubs using several surface materials, including pine bark mulch, bare soil, and turfgrass. On a square-foot basis, plants mulched daily lost more water than unmulched plants, the report said.

Please don't take this study too seriously and decide not to mulch. Three or four inches of bark chips *does* cut down on water loss, as does a newspaper mulch, straw, hay, and so on. An unmulched soil surface gets heat from the sun, dries out quickly, heats up fast, and lacks the beauty of mulch around the plant, to say nothing of the weeds that are kept out of mulched beds.

If mulching is a foolish practice, how come saw mills have such a hard time keeping up with the demand from landscapers and gardeners? To us, the use of mulches is one of the greatest ideas to spread in the past 50 years. Don't give up mulching. It saves you money, hard work, and a lot of frustration. If there's proof to the contrary, then thousands of landscapers don't know what they're doing! And that includes us.

Wood wastes such as shredded bark, sawdust, and wood chips should not be used as mulch because they turn sour and injure plants.

These waste materials are perfectly safe and should be used to conserve moisture, cut down on weeds, improve soil, and improve the looks around trees and shrubs. Once in a while, however, these materials turn sour or toxic. We'll explain why.

Plants are injured by nonliving or abiotic conditions. In other words, souring is not caused by agents such as fungal spores, bacteria, nematodes, or insects. Diagnosis of mulch toxicity is a bit tricky because symptoms resemble those caused by drought, excess water, chemical injury, and fertilizer burn.

When a mulch material is stacked in a pile, decomposition takes place and methane, alcohol, ammonia, or hydrogen sulfide gas can build to toxic levels. These toxic by-products develop under anaerobic conditions, or without oxygen present. Anaerobic conditions can occur in large compost piles having pockets without oxygen, such as saturated piles (where water content is greater than 40%) and in piles that are not turned frequently. If the composting process is allowed to continue until maturity, the harmful by-products will disappear. But if you apply an immature compost containing any of these toxic gases or alcohol, plants can develop symptoms of mulch toxicity within 24 hours.

Symptoms include marginal leaf chlorosis, leaf scorch, leafdrop, or plant death. Dropped on grass, immature compost will cause yellowing or scorching. To avoid problems, use only well-aged mulch or mulch from small piles, or let a truckload of mulch sit for a week before spreading.

Wood chips around trees or shrubs attract ants and fungi, and cause yellowing of plants. They also make the soil acid.

False. Stockpile all the chips you can get. Peat moss makes the soil more acidic; compost is usually neutral; manure is slightly alkaline and makes the soil more alkaline. Some wood chips (e.g., pine chips) can increase acidity slightly. However, to make them useful they must be treated with a little extra nitrogen. As you know, soil microbes break down any organic matter, and the activity is affected by the amount of carbon and nitrogen in the organic waste. This is called the C:N ratio. Because microbes need a certain amount of nitrogen for their own use (growth), they may deplete soil nitrogen levels in the process of breaking down fresh wood chips or sawdust. Materials high in carbon (e.g., straw, sawdust, or wood chips) will decompose very slowly unless nitrogen fertilizer is added.

Tree leaves are higher in nitrogen than straw or sawdust. Grass clippings are high in nitrogen and when mixed with leaves or sawdust will help decomposition.

We should "bark" or mulch trees every year.

It's not necessary to do it every year. Mulched trees may have as much as 90 percent more roots than trees growing without it. Keep the mulch depth at about 4 inches (10 cm). (If you apply a 6-inch (15 cm) layer, it will settle to the 4-inch (10 cm) optimum depth.) Refresh the mulch as it settles or decomposes. This may be yearly or it may be less often. As the tree grows, consider extending the size of the mulched area. Mulching the area under the tree's drip zone should cover much of the tree's roots.

Just a word of caution: Although we sing the praises of mulching, we can often overdo it, producing what is known as "mulch poisoning." This is the result of piling or mounding 12 inches (30 cm) or so of a material around a tree or shrub. Too heavy a mulch can cause damaging by-products to form. To prevent this, do not mound mulch over 6 inches. Leave a small depression around the trunk or stems so air can get down into the area.

Oak leaves should be used as mulch for acid-loving plants because they make the soil acidic.

Oak leaves are often singled out as beneficial for the acid-loving crops but they are not as acidic as many others. Most leaves are acidic (with a pH below 6), but that's not bad. As leaves break down in the soil, changes do take place, but it seldom changes the soil acidity enough to harm plants. Even loads of leaves rarely change the acidity to below 6.5, which is fine for most vegetables and ornamentals.

What's really important is that the organic matter in leaves has a buffering effect that prevents too big a change in acidity or alkalinity. Compost your leaves in a pile large enough to hold heat. Rake them as soon as they've fallen. Leaves that sit for weeks, unraked, dry out. Put them in a pile 6 by 6 feet and let the heat of microbial activity help break them down. You can either mow over leaves with a lawnmower to chop before composting, or till leaves (preferably chopped) into the garden in the fall.

Well-rotted leaves are not highly acidic, as the books say. Use all you can get your hands on, regardless of what kind they are.

The old-fashioned practice of making organic tea for fertilizer was a waste of time.

Not necessarily. It refers to a tea made of compost or manure that can be used as a soluble fertilizer for your vegetables and flowers. This fertilizer is very quickly taken up, almost as quickly as a soluble synthetic fertilizer. If you have ever made sun tea, then you can make organic tea.

Simply take a cupful or two of compost or manure and place it in a burlap sack. If you don't have burlap, use old pantyhose or a sock — anything that allows water to flow through without allowing the compost to escape. Place the compost-filled bag in a container capable of holding 2 to 3 gallons (7.6 –11.4 liters) of water. Fill with water, cover, and place in a sunny location for 2 days. At the end of that time, remove the bag and you have a nice tea. Be careful if you use fresh manure, since the solution may be very strong and even capable of burning plants due to the high nitrogen content. (Did you notice an ammonia smell when you removed the cover?) Dilute the tea until it becomes very lightly colored. Now you are ready to use it as you would any soluble fertilizer.

Newspaper logs give off a gas.

Don't worry about newspapers giving off deadly gases or toxic materials. It's a good business to make and burn newspaper logs. The more paper we keep out of plastic garbage bags, the better off we all are. A cord of newspaper logs contains almost the same amount of BTU's (heat units) found in a cord of hardwood.

It's not a good idea to use wood ashes in your garden because they contain radiation.

Don't believe what you hear about radiation and wood ashes. Wood ashes are safe to use, and gardeners should have no fear of using them on vegetable gardens even though they do contain naturally occurring radioactive isotope Potassium 40 (K40). This is a fact of nature that cannot be avoided. All living things on earth contain K40, a compound that's been around since "day one" and is necessary for the existence of life. Potassium is needed for growth, and that is why it is one of the "big three" in fertilizers.

Note: In certain amounts, wood ashes act like a key and unlock soil nutrients so plants can take them up. Very large quantities of wood ashes may make soil too alkaline, but you can check for this with a soil test.

Fallen leaves along the roadside should not be used on the garden because they contain lead or other deposits from automobile exhaust systems.

Perhaps some lead or other pollutants do fall on the leaves, but it's not enough to worry about. The practice of hauling leaves to the dump should be stopped. Leaves should be composted or dumped on the garden because the humus content of a ton of leaves is unbelievable. Your soil needs all the leaf mold it can get because this rotted material has a miraculous ability to hold moisture and nutrients. Subsoil can hold a mere 20 percent of its weight in water; good top-soil will hold 60 percent; and leaf mold can retain 300 to 500 percent. Pound for pound, the leaves of most of our common trees contain twice as many nutrients as manure, including nutrients such as calcium, phosphorus, and magnesium. Tests at Cornell Univesity show that organic matter actually slows down the uptake of lead in vegetable gardens near busy roads.

11.
Insects
and Pesticides

Lightning bugs (also called "fireflies") cause damage to plants.

False. The fireflies you see flying on summer evenings are all males looking for lady friends. The female does not have wings. She has a grublike appearance and is often called a "glowworm." Her light is bluer and dimmer than her male counterpart's. The female waits in the grass flashing her light to attract males. There is a predatory species of firefly that waits in the grass mimicking the female's sequence of flashes. When the male lands to mate, it's eaten instead. Light given off by the fireflies is cold light. There is no heat to it. The light comes from the oxidation of an enzyme, a reaction that's efficient in making light.

Fireflies do not damage plants. In fact, some are important allies because their larvae eat eggs of slugs and grasshoppers, as well as some small maggots and caterpillars.

Houseplants attract fleas.

Most people who grow houseplants usually have a cat or dog in the household. As a result, some think there is a connection between fleas and plants. Insects that bother pets don't bother plants and vice versa. Houseplants get "plant lice" or aphids, which thrive on plant juices only. Fleas on cats and dogs live on blood. Animal fleas are tougher to combat. Most plant pests can be kept under control with soap suds, but fleas on animals succeed because they overwhelm evolutionary laws with sheer volume. If your cat or dog brings 10 female fleas into the house, within a month you'll be hosting 2,000 adult fleas, 90,000 eggs, and 175,000 fleas in larval (worm) and pupal (resting) stages. The larval flea is a little maggotlike creature that eats blood proteins in adult-flea fecal matter. Flashing light or vibrations cause the pupae to hatch out in an explosion of hungry beasts. You may have experienced this phenomenon if you've walked into an infested house that has been vacant for a few weeks. As you walk, movements trigger massive hatching sprees and your legs become covered with fleas.

Plant pests are easy to control, but there is no easy solution to fighting animal fleas. We've learned over the years that one of the best weapons for controlling fleas is your vacuum cleaner. It picks up eggs, fleas, and larvae as well as flea feces, the larval food. Vacuum cleaner vibrations will stimulate the resting stages to hatch and adult fleas can be more easily picked up. If you vacuum a flea-infested house, squirt some pesticide in the bag, or use moth flakes because the container could become a breeding ground for more fleas. Burn the bag immediately when finished.

Combing your pet daily helps to control fleas. Rubbing orange and grapefruit rinds on fur also helps.

Vitamin A and garlic tablets will keep mosquitoes away.

We know of no folk remedies that dissuade mosquitoes. A lotion sold by Avon, Skin-So-Soft, seems to act as a mild repellent, but nothing is better than wearing long pants and a long-sleeved shirt. Some people rub orange peel over their skin before working in a garden, and it helps.

Mosquitoes are more likely to bite men than women, and they tend to be less interested in infants and people over 60.

Mosquitoes use warmth and moisture to seek you out, flying upwind until they get to the source. Only the females "bite," and they prefer to lunch on people who are hot and sweaty, over those who keep cool and dry. Carbon dioxide and lactic acid are attractants, and some people produce more than others. Dark clothes and dark skin seem more attractive. Some people also react more to a bite than others.

Mosquitoes breed in stagnant pools of water, so make sure there are no containers filled with water near your garden.

Electric bug zappers are a good way to eliminate pesky mosquitoes.

People who have studied the effects of bug zappers tell us they do more harm than good. A recent article in *Bird Watcher's Digest* supported that. Listening to the evening songs of birds is one of the best parts of life. Unfortunately one is likely also to hear snap, crackle, and pop sounds coming from a neighbor's yard. It's the sound of many good insects being electrocuted.

We got rid of our bug zapper after studying what kind of insects it kills. First, people think that all night-flying insects are bad and must be eliminated. But 99 percent of the insects on this planet are harmless or even actually benefit humans. People remember the nasty ones, attract them to a light source, and "zap" them on a charged grid.

We thought bug zappers attract and kill mosquitoes. David Donnelly, who studied the problem, says there's nothing further from the truth. Two reasons why insects are attracted to light: (1) Many night-flying insects use the natural light of the moon and stars as a navigational aid.

Donnelly says that when insects come across an artificial light, they get confused and buzz around it. (2) Some insects use light to find a mate, such as fireflies signaling each other in courtship. Mosquitoes flying at night do not use light. They go after you because you are a mammal giving off carbon dioxide; the smell of it is what the mosquitoes home in on. Bug zappers kill insects that prey on mosquitoes — for example, crane flies, which look like large mosquitoes. They use light as a guide and are killed by the hundreds by a bug zapper. Crane flies dine on mosquitoes.

Your best defense against mosquitoes is the bat: It uses radar and can find and eat mosquitoes at the rate of more than 500 per hour! Instead of spending money on a bug zapper, why not install a box for hosting and breeding bats? Meanwhile, if you have a neighbor who is impressed by the snap, crackle, and pop coming from a bug zapper, enlighten the person about the uselessness of the device and about the harm it does to the environment. Bats are a much better alternative for coping with mosquitoes.

There are mosquito-repelling plants that can be grown in pots on decks and patios and used to repel the pests.

False! Let's start by saying there are dozens of plants that produce essential oils in their leaves that repel various insect pests, including mosquitoes. However, we know of no plants that produce oils strong enough to repel mosquitoes any farther away than the surface of their leaves. It is a fallacy to think that plants "squirt" enough aroma to repel mosquitoes significantly.

If you rub the leaves of certain plants on your skin, however, the aroma can repel insects. You may have some of these plants growing right on your own property: rosemary *(Rosemarinus officinalis)*, scented geranium cultivars, basil *(Ocimum)*, to name a few. Don't spend a lot of money on some "exotic" plant that is advertised to keep your backyard, patio, or deck free from insects, including mosquitoes.

A very cold winter will kill bugs and worms in my garden, so there'll be fewer bugs the following year.

If you think that cold weather kills bugs, you're mistaken. Insects are tough and will take all the cold that Mother Nature can give them. Some species carry their own

INSECTS, BUGS, LIVING WELL UNDER BOB'S GARDEN DURING HARD WINTER

BUG A BOO

BUGGIE

antifreeze in them. Their bloodstreams contain as much as 50 percent glycerol, a natural antifreeze. Some species lose water in their bodies when winter sets in, enabling them to hibernate without danger of freezing. Other insects head south for the winter.

How does a brutal winter affect plant diseases? Most plant diseases are immune to cold weather, although we understand that the cold weather will kill powdery mildew on cherry and apple trees. If that is true, it could be helpful to people who do not want to spray.

Temperature has nothing to do with the growth of insects.

False. The hotter it gets, the hotter an insect gets. When hot weather hits, insect populations explode. In short, the reason for this is that insect development is related to temperature. As temperatures increase, the time for insects to complete their life cycle decreases. We'll cite some examples: Thrips, which take 57 days to develop from egg to adult when the air temperature is 54°F (12°C), take only 12 days to complete the cycle when air temperature is 77°F (25°C).

With spider mites, the effect of temperature is more dramatic. Mites take 30 days to complete the egg-to-adult life cycle at 60°F (16°C), 21 days at 64°F (18°C), 14.5 days at 70°F (21°C), and only 3.5 days at 86°F (30°C). This relationship also applies to whiteflies. The natural life cycle of the sweet potato whitefly varies from 18 to 57 days, depending on temperatures and food sources. In a 65° to 75°F (18°–24°C) home or greenhouse, the life cycle averages 39 days. The common greenhouse whitefly's life cycle averages 32 days.

Remember, the hotter it gets, the faster insects multiply. Be on your toes and check for bugs before they get a chance to have a population explosion.

To get rid of houseplant pests you have to use commercial insecticides.

False. Rinsing leaves under a strong stream of water takes care of many pests. For persistent plant pests, mix 1 teaspoon (5 ml) of liquid dishwashing detergent, 1 cup (250 ml) of vegetable oil, and shake vigorously to emulsify. Add this to 1 quart (1 liter) of tap water, and apply at 10-day intervals. Or use commercial insecticidal soaps. For sensitive houseplants such as ferns, test on a leaf and wait 2 days. If there is no leaf damage, you can spray the whole plant.

Earthworms are a nuisance in the lawn and garden. They make mounds of soil and prevent grass from growing.

Let the worms work for you. Earthworm castings contain 5 times the nitrate, 7 times the phosphorus, 3 times the exchangeable magnesium, 11 times the potash, and 1½ times the calcium found in the best topsoil in the United States.

The rich earth of the Nile delta is one of the reasons that ancient Egyptian civilization flourished for 3,000 years. Billions of earthworms produced the great fertility of the soil in that valley, converting the annual alluvial deposits into a soil of exceptional richness. There are about 90,000 earthworms in every good acre of soil, but some could have a population of 3 million to the acre.

Earthworms are beneficial, aerating the soil and recycling organic matter. If you eliminated earthworms from your lawn, thatch (a layer of live and dead plant tissue on the soil surface) would build up and your grass would probably dry up even though it got plenty of water. Tests show that where pesticides drive out or kill earthworms, thatch sheds water, causing it to run off instead of in. That's because earthworms aren't there to break it down.

Charles Darwin noticed more than a century ago that earthworms were a big help in "churning" fields. Apply this fact to your lawn: About 30 tons of organic residues per acre are consumed by earthworms annually and converted into nutrients that plants need. Even on strip mining soil banks in Ohio, as much as 2 tons of debris is consumed by earthworms, which help improve the soil. The fertile castings of soil and feces passed by the earthworm are really good for your lawn. They can be an obstruction on a golf course, but on your lawn they should be regarded as a boon.

I know very little about a material called "diatomaceous earth" for controlling slugs and snails. If it kills slugs, won't it kill earthworms also?

No. Diatomaceous earth is an abrasive dust with razor-sharp particles formed from the fossil remains of prehistoric algae. Its abrasive effect causes the slugs to dehydrate by losing too much water. It appears to be completely digestible by earthworms. Diatomaceous earth is also harmless to birds, bees, and mammals. It even contains a number of beneficial trace minerals and is a component in some commercial insecticides. You can buy the material in any garden store. Scatter the material around the base of your plants — slugs absolutely won't go through it!

Those "inert" ingredients in pesticides are safe and harmless.

Don't bet on it. The term "inert" is misleading. They are a "carrier" or a "filler" for an active ingredient in a formulation. If you check several spray or dust preparations, you may find the labels to show the inerts accounting for from 50 to 99.9 percent of a formula. These "inert" ingredients in pesticides could be more harmful than the active chemicals. They are added to dilute, preserve, dye, or help make a pesticide stick to foliage better. It's not possible to use a chemical in its pure form because it takes only a small amount to do the job. The same is true of chemical fertilizers. They contain inert fillers such as sand and vermiculite because the chemicals would kill the plants if used undiluted.

A lot of the residue you see on fruits and vegetables could be one of the inert materials used. Wash or scrub off any residues you see, and even if you don't notice any, be sure to wash your produce.

Soap solution is useless as a pesticide.

Soap solutions have been used for years to control mealy bugs and other insects on houseplants. Safer's Insecticidal Soap, sold commercially, leaves little or no visible residue on foliage when dry. Some gardeners shred Fels Naptha soap and dissolve one-half bar in 2 gallons (7.6 liters) of water. Heat the mixture to dissolve the soap completely. This cooled solution can be sprayed on infested plants, where it will leave little visible residue. Fels Naptha is a laundry soap sold in most grocery stores. Try the soap spray on one test plant first.

I would like a good fungicide but can't find any safe ones. I heard a homemade formula is available but it does not work on houseplants and roses.

Here is a homemade formula for combating mildew on houseplants and black spot on roses: Use 1 tablespoon (15 ml) each of baking soda and dishwashing detergent (such as Ivory or Joy), mix together, and add it to 1 gallon (3.8 liters) of water. Spray this on the foliage of houseplants in the morning so the leaves are dry by nightfall. For black spot on roses, start using the formula soon after the leaves start to open up, repeating once a week.

You need high-powered fungicides to control blight on tomatoes and potatoes.

You can spray tomatoes and potatoes weekly with a simple organic fungicide called "Cornell Formula": mix 1 tablespoon (15 ml) each of light horticultural oil and baking soda in 1 gallon (3.8 liters) of water. Spray it on the plants before blight strikes. Rotating crops will greatly reduce problems with blight on tomatoes and potatoes. Avoid planting either where tomatoes or potatoes were grown in the past 3 years.

It's impossible to grow a good garden without using a lot of pesticides.

You can grow good vegetables without reaching for the flit gun every 5 minutes. Sometimes pesticides may be needed to gain control of certain damaging insect problems, but in most cases it's wiser to do nothing or to use alternatives to traditional chemicals.

We're encouraged that many gardeners avoid plastering plants with pesticides as a first resort against garden pests. We can accept the fact that insects are a natural part of a diverse landscape, and losing a few leaves on a plant isn't a disaster. If you've got two or three caterpillars on a hedge, it really doesn't mean you have to haul out the pesticide gun. We have to get used to less-than-perfect crops. Fewer and fewer pesticides are available to homeowners today.

We have devised a number of good household remedies for coping with insects. In many cases, remedies you make yourself work just as well as the high-powered pesticides. The hot pepper formulations are effective on a number of pests in the adult, larval, and other immature stages, as well as for keeping rabbits, deer, woodchucks, and chipmunks away from flowers and vegetables.

Even organic sprays (such as hot pepper) can be irritating to eyes and nose. Do not breathe the fumes and do not spray on a windy day.

✔ **Liquid Detergent Alcohol Spray.** Mix 1 teaspoon (5 ml) of liquid dishwashing detergent (any well-known brand *but not automatic dishwasher detergent)* plus 1 pint (50 ml) of rubbing alcohol (around 70% isopropyl) in 1 quart (1 liter) of water. Test on a few leaves first to make sure it won't harm sensitive plants. Spray top and bottom sides of leaves; or if plant is small and is potted, invert it in a large pan of solution (holding soil ball securely) and gently swish back and forth. Repeat in 7 days.

✔ **Liquid Detergent–Hot Pepper Spray.** Steep 3 tablespoons (45 ml) dry, crushed hot peppers in ½ cup (140 ml) hot water for a half hour. Strain out the peppers and mix solution with the liquid detergent formula mentioned above. Good for a number of insects bothering both indoor and outdoor plants. **Note:** Move plants outdoors to apply. Do not use on a windy day. Avoid breathing fumes. Can cause irritation to nose and eyes.

✔ **Liquid Detergent–Hot Pepper–Garlic Spray.** Steep 2 tablespoons (30 ml) dry crushed hot peppers and 3 cloves garlic in ½ cup (140 ml) hot water for a half hour. Strain into quart (liter) jar and fill remainder of jar with the liquid detergent formula mentioned above. **Note:** Move plants outdoors to apply.

✔ **Liquid Detergent–Hot Pepper–Mineral Oil Spray.** To Liquid Detergent–Hot Pepper Spray, add 1 tablespoon (15 ml) of mineral oil. Mix well. If hot pepper sprays are used on leafy vegetables, be sure to wash leaves before serving to remove the hot taste.

✔ **Murphy's Oil Soap Spray.** Use at a rate of ¼ cup (70 ml) per gallon (3.8 liters) of warm water. Kills whiteflies, mites, aphids, scale, and others.

✔ **USDA Spray:** Mix 2 teaspoons (10 ml) of liquid dishwashing detergent with 1 cup (280 ml) of vegetable oil (peanut oil, safflower, and so on). Shake vigorously to emulsify, and add to a quart (liter) of tap water. Use at 10-day intervals as an all-purpose spray on any plant.

The following are sprays for specific insect pests:

✔ **Mealy Bugs.** Use rubbing alcohol right from the bottle. A cotton ball or soft cloth soaked with the solution can be used to wash off areas of infestation. Or use Rubbing Alcohol–Hot Pepper Spray: Steep 2 tablespoons (30 ml) of crushed dried hot peppers in 1 cup (280 ml) of hot water for half an hour. Strain into sprayer. Add an equal amount of rubbing alcohol. This can be sprayed on plants, covering all areas, or can be used to wash plants with a soft cloth or soft toothbrush. Be sure to get into crevices.

✔ **Scale Control.** Use buttermilk or sour milk. Soak cloth or paint brush with either material and dab on infestation. Later, rub off insects and dispose of them in a sealed bag in case any are alive. Or try rubbing alcohol — it soaks through the shell, hitting the enclosed insect. If only a few scales are present, lift them off with a pair of tweezers.

✔ **Spider Mites.** Spray frequently with liquid detergent in water. Liquid Detergent–Hot Pepper–Mineral Oil formula works well if repeated at 7-day intervals until mites are gone. A Buttermilk–Wheat Flour formula is a good cure, but it may leave a white residue that is hard to remove. Mix ¼ cup (70 ml) buttermilk, 2 cups (560 ml) wheat flour, and 2½ gallons (9.5 liters) water. Mix flour and water so it isn't lumpy. Strain the solution so it doesn't clog sprayer. Shake each time you spray.

✔ **Aphids.** Use Liquid Detergent–Hot Pepper Spray, USDA Spray, or a commercial insecticidal soap.

✔ **Whiteflies.** Spread heavy motor oil or molasses on a piece of yellow cardboard and hang over plants. The yellow color will attract the whiteflies. To spray, use the Liquid Detergent–Hot Pepper–Mineral Oil formula.

Remember, no spray is perfect. Of these safe formulas you can make right in your own home some are all-purpose, some are for certain insects. Remember that well-nourished plants have more protection aginst insects, just as healthy people have greater disease resistance.

Note: Try any of these home sprays on a few test leaves and wait a couple of days before spraying the whole plant. Various factors can cause injury, such as brands, water pH, and sensitivity of particular plants (e.g., ferns).

We are organic gardeners and do not like to use sprays unless they are made from plants. We feel those are perfectly safe. Are we correct?

Pesticides made from plants are called "botanicals." These include rotenone and pyrethrin, which have been accepted by some growers and certifying groups as organic and thus safe. They are safer than certain synthetic chemicals, but they are still toxic to beneficial insects and some animals and should be treated like any pesticide.

Like most pesticides, many botanicals contain "inert ingredients," some of which retain toxicity for a shorter period. They may also affect beneficial insects. Use the botanicals with the same care you would use with any other pesticide.

12.
The Birds
and the Bees

In the winter, birds can fend for themselves by eating weed seeds.

False! If you want fewer insects around your home in summer, feed birds in winter. Birds are the best pest control you can get. For the record, one bird fed on 217 fall webworms at a single sitting. Seven cedar waxwings felt no pain after gulping 100 cankerworms. Birds are among your garden's best friends and it is very easy to attract them. Feed them in winter and they will reward you in summer.

By the way, if someone says, "You eat like a bird" — that's no compliment! Ounce for ounce, nothing in the animal kingdom eats as much or as frequently as do birds in your garden. And remember, birds not only feed themselves, but from dawn to dusk bird parents struggle to fill four, five, or six yawning little pink gullets with grubs, bugs, and such.

Enjoy your birds in winter and feed them regularly. It is not money wasted!

It is a good practice to feed stale bread to birds.

Experts say that feeding bread scraps to birds in winter can be harmful. Bread doesn't provide enough nutrition for birds in winter.

The bird population can be divided into two basic groups: hard-billed seed-eaters, whose diet is mainly seed, and soft-billed insect eaters. Both types like suet. The best bird food you can provide is sunflower seeds or the regular wild-bird mix found in garden centers or hardware stores. (Avoid the cheap mixes that contain a lot of red milo, which birds do not eat.)

Note: Don't use metal food containers or screens in winter, there's a chance the birds might get their eyes or tongues stuck to the cold metal. Wire will do the same. Instead, use plastic-coated wire, wood, or plastic, or use plastic onion sacks for suet.

Birds are fatter in winter because they have extra body weight to endure the cold.

Backyard birds *look* fatter in winter, but that's because they are fluffing up their feathers to trap air and keep themselves warm. During hot weather, birds will hold their feathers close to their bodies, making them look thin.

Feathers are what make a bird a bird — from the hummingbird's 1,500 to the swan's 25,000. Insulation of a bird's body is the main function of down feathers. Being one of the strongest yet lightest materials "manufactured" by any animal, feathers are remarkable for their shapes, colors, and insulating qualities.

Is sunflower seed the best single food for birds? We are told you shouldn't use a mixture because the ingredients are inferior.

Birdseed mixtures are not in themselves poor, although some have millet, which most birds reject. Many mixes are excellent. Safflower is often included in a quality seed mix. (Some say squirrels do not like safflower, but chipmunks love it.)

Niger thistle is a high-calorie gourmet birdfood imported from Africa. It's quite expensive, but if you love finches you won't mind the high price. Mourning doves and many native sparrows clean up spillage in a hurry. Although it is called "thistle," it is not a true thistle and will not germinate in your backyard.

The cheaper birdseed mixes found in grocery stores or discount places are just as good as the higher priced mixes.

Very often the bags of mixed seeds you find in grocery stores or discount stores are cheaper, but that doesn't mean they are a bargain. Quite often they are laced with oats, wheat, milo, and other filler grains that most birds refuse to eat. Few birds visit the feeders having these cheap mixes, and the ground beneath sprouts a crop of oats, wheat, and other grains in the spring.

Shop carefully and you will find some excellent seed mixes available, costing a bit more per bag but with little waste. You can judge the quality by reading the ingredients on the label. Sunflower seed should always be listed first, followed by other good seeds such as safflower and white millet.

Can you blend your own seed mix? Sure. Buy bags of individual seeds and start out with something like this: 50 percent black-oil sunflower seed, 20 percent striped sunflower seed, 15 percent white millet, and 15 percent safflower.

Black-oil sunflower seed ranks as the best single food you can offer birds. Seeds are thin-shelled, easy to open, and rich in fat and protein. Almost every bird that comes to your backyard feeder will eat black-oil seeds. Striped sunflower seeds are larger and have thicker shells than black-oil seeds. Cardinals, blue jays, tufted titmice, and red-bellied wood-peckers go for striped sunflower seeds.

Note: Avoid hulled sunflower seeds — they cost more and are apt to spoil quickly when wet.

Is it a good idea to buy lady beetles in gallon lots to release them in your greenhouse and garden?

Most beetles take flight a short time after being released, so it is probably not gardening money wisely spent.

If you see some lady beetles in your home, don't destroy them! This aphid killer is unusual because it overwinters in massive mountain clusters in California, allowing collectors to harvest and package large numbers for sale in nurseries and through garden supply catalogs and other outlets through the country. In case someone asks you, its name is *Hippodamia convergens*, order Coleoptera and family Coccinellidae — a real friend to have in the home or the

garden. When they run out of aphids (plant lice) they either feed on themselves or move on. Does it pay to buy the beetles in gallon lots and disperse them in your greenhouse or garden? Probably not!

There are more songbirds than ever before.

The Smithsonian Institution in Washington tells us that populations of many birds are *declining* at rates of 1 percent to 4 percent a year. A number of scientists say the cause is the American appetite for "fast food" such as hamburgers and frankfurters. Since the U.S. government authorized imports of cheap beef from Central and South America, vast areas of rainforests — over 11 million acres a year — have been felled to make cattle pastures. That now represents over 60 percent of tropical rainforests. At the present rate of destruction, no forests will be left. The billions of birds of more than 150 species that migrate each fall to these forests have disappeared in the last 30 years, and fewer and fewer warblers, tanagers, peewees, vireos, kingbirds, and others make the trip.

Birds peck at a window or crash into them because they're jealous of the image they see.

Some birds, especially male cardinals and robins, are notorious for pecking on a window. They are aggressive, especially during the nesting season, and often spend 90 percent of their time chasing away other males. When they peck on a window they are seeing their own reflection and, thinking it's another male, are trying to get at it. In short, the male bird does not want another male lover around; he fights for his territorial rights.

When birds fly into a window, it's another thing. Apparently they don't see the glass and will fly into it, often killing themselves. Decals of hawk silhouettes are available to affix to window panes to prevent this.

Lint, yarn, or fabric should be put out so birds can use it for nesting.

False. These materials hold water, increasing the chance of baby birds contracting respiratory disease. Hair (dog or other animal), straw, and other natural (to birds) nesting materials are not absorbent and will shed rain quickly. The Audubon Society has had warnings out regarding this for a couple of years now.

We want to attract more butterflies. I heard that if we put up a colorful butterfly feeder, complete with nectar, it would bring on butterflies. Does the nectar solution attract insects such as wasps, and is it sanitary?

Save your money. According to Beth Yagodzinski, laboratory manager of Butterfly World in Florida, if you want to attract butterflies you'd be better advised to put your money into a few nursery plants with proven butterfly appeal, such as bee balm. Given a choice between feeders and plants, butterflies always choose the plants and ignore the feeders.

We do not recommend that you put out a butterfly feeder, because bacteria can easily grow in the feeders. And commercial nectars are full of artificial colorants.

Some butterflies enjoy rotting fruit. Put your windfall apples and pears on a plate or piece of wood, high enough off the ground to discourage pouncing cats. Some gardeners avoid doing this because rotting fruit attracts wasps and ants, which may discourage butterflies from landing. Go ahead and experiment.

Human warts can be caused by handling toads.

Toads may look like a prehistoric animal from another world, and although some still believe they cause warts, human warts are caused by a virus that has nothing to do with toads. Warts can spread from one part of the body to another or from one person to another, but not from toads. Anyone who has toads is very fortunate. They are great bug catchers.

Toads are poisonous and can exude a toxic chemical.

They are not poisonous. They are valuable bug killers. An entomologist figured that a single toad is worth $200 to $300 in bug control today. Toads eat all kinds of injurious beetles, sowbugs, slugs and snails, potato beetles, grasshoppers, caterpillars, armyworms, wireworms, and gypsy moths. About 80 percent of the toad's diet consists of pest insects. One lone toad will eat tens of thousands of insects a year — up to three times its weight in pests. They are strictly nonvege-

tarian. They have a sticky tongue, which is one "insecticide" no insect can develop resistance to.

Toads even eat cucumber beetles, which feed on cucumber plants. The cucumber plants contain a naturally bitter chemical known as curcurbitacin, making the beetles bitter, too. This insect is avoided by predators because it tastes so bad, yet toads gobble up these bitter-tasting beetles.

Moles and voles cause untold damage to lawns. Pesticides are the best way to cope with them since they are not beneficial in any way.

Over 98 percent of the diet of moles is grubs, insects, and worms. They do little or no damage to plant roots. Most of the damage is done by voles or meadow mice. Hot Tabasco sauce, ½ ounce (15 ml), plus 1 teaspoon (5 ml) of chili powder added to a pint of water with a little dish detergent will discourage them. Pour or put a little in the runways.

As bad as voles are, many conservationists feel voles have a purpose in life. They are an important food source for many predators such as the barn owl, which has a specific diet consisting mostly of meadow voles. The barn owl is an endangered species in some areas, due to decreasing habitat and numbers of meadow voles. That may not be comforting to gardeners whose fruit trees are girdled by voles.

Moles eat bulbs and roots.

False. People have a false notion as to the damage moles do. They do *not* munch on bulbs or roots, but they *do* make tunnels in the soil in search of grubs and earthworms. When you see mole tunnels and missing bulbs or damaged plants, you should suspect field mice and voles (that is voles, not moles). These rodents use mole tunnels for protection and as avenues to food supplies.

A mole has a tremendous appetite and can eat half its own weight in food daily. The common mole has broad, shovel-like front feet. Moles stay underground, seldom venturing out of their burrows. They are most active early in the morning and late in the evening. They give themselves away by making above-ground ridges. Roll the ridges with a lawn roller and grass will come up again.

There is no need to control them. If you kill off their food (grubs), they go elsewhere. Fighting them with traps is tricky because moles are very suspicious and will avoid traps. Baits can be used for *voles,* but moles seldom have any interest in bait.

If you don't like their tunnels, control moles by controlling the grubs that attract them to your lawn. You can purchase predatory nematodes at garden centers that will get rid of the moles' food supply — thus no more moles.

13.
Miscellaneous

Goldenrod causes hay fever.

Goldenrod has long been shunned by North American gardeners for its supposed allergic effects. The true culprit, however, is ragweed, a common goldenrod companion whose lighter, windborne pollen is a common allergen.

As interest in creating habitats for birds and insects has grown, goldenrod's usefulness as a late-blooming source of nectar has not gone unnoted. Many nursery catalogs sell goldenrod plants. Most bloom from midsummer into autumn, combining comfortably with old roadside favorites such as rosy Joe-Pye weed *(Eupatorium maculatum)*, pale gray boneset *(E. perfoliatum)*, and fluffy white snakeroot *(E. rugosum)*. None of these are common allergens, but it is said that snakeroot *(E. rugosum)* is the plant that killed Abraham Lincoln's mother. She died from drinking milk from a cow that had eaten snakeroot. But that's no reason why you shouldn't enjoy its great potential.

Gardening has no health benefits for the gardener.

General gardening work burns about 220 calories per hour. Naturally, activities such as hoeing, digging potatoes, and pushing a lawnmower burn more calories than transplanting seedlings. Unlike many sports, gardening can be a lifetime activity. You can even garden in a wheelchair. Besides the exercise involved in gardening, it's next to impossible to grow anything in your garden that is not low in calories and high in fiber. The garden is a great place to relieve stress. Looking at the details of a beautiful flower or stopping to enjoy the fragrance of a rose can be calming. And lashing out at a weed is better than lashing out at your spouse or children.

Gardeners always like to predict the weather, but they are seldom right.

Gardeners have their own way of making predictions about the weather, and we believe they are right more than they are wrong. They seem to develop a natural ability to predict the weather accurately.

There's a lot of truth to those old sayings, such as "Red sky at night, sailor's delight; red sky in the morning, sailor take warning." Or maybe you have heard the saying: "Evening red and morning gray, send the traveler on his way." When the atmosphere is dusty, it transmits the sun's red rays instead of the blue as the sun nears the horizon. Basically, when the sun is red and the sky clear at sunset, we get the message that there are no clouds for a long distance in the west. Since most storms and weather fronts move in from the west, bad weather is nowhere near us. Gardeners learn from years of forecasting, and they can be at least 75 percent right. Meteorologists with all their technical know-how are about 85 percent correct.

Home gardeners use caterpillars to predict weather, and they are all environmental weirdos.

Not necessarily. Home gardeners often use caterpillars (woolly wormlike stage of butterflies and moths) to predict or forecast nature's weather. My wife is a "caterpillarian," having studied the hairy black and brown caterpillars known

as woolly bears. They are the larval stage of the common tiger moth, with a wide, light brown band around the middle. My wife says that when the woolly bear grows a heavy coat, it's going to be a tough winter. Also, if the woolly bear has a wide, light brown band, a mild winter is in store. The wider the band, the milder the winter. If the caterpillar is mostly black and has a narrow brown band, you'd better go to yard sales and buy all the winter underwear you can get for a severe winter.

How accurate is the woolly bear business? There's no scientific fact to back up the woolly bear forecasters, but old-timers who've studied it for years say it's fairly accurate.

Forecasting weather by observing animals is pure superstition.

Not at all. Weather forecasting (meteorology) is an inexact science; after all, the planet is traveling at 18 miles per second. Maybe forecasters should observe animals once in a while and use it along with studies of the atmosphere. Old-time gardeners tell you that a variety of animals can foretell weather changes on a short-term basis. Here are a few examples of animal behavior that are said to foretell weather:

✔ Migratory birds, even bats, will soar in good weather, but stay low or close to the ground and roost before a storm.
✔ If migrating geese fly due north or south, you can expect fair weather the next day. But if they fly east to west, get out your raincoat.
✔ Bees can tell when a summer rainstorm is due, and they prefer to stay close to the hive.
✔ Cows and deer stand facing east if good weather is due and west if it's not.
✔ Good gardening weather can be expected if you see ants or spiders engaged in lots of activity.
✔ Expect rain if flies are biting more often and more severely than usual.
✔ Crickets can give you the approximate temperature. Count the number of chirps registered in 14 seconds and add 40; the total will be the present air temperature in degrees Fahrenheit.

Lightning will not strike a tree twice.

It will strike a tree or anything else once, twice, or many times. The greatest danger occurs when a tall tree is growing in shallow soil over rocks, which forces the current to spread out sideways over the soil. Needless to say, under a tree is the worst place in the world to hide during a thunderstorm.

You can look at a plant (or plant parts) and tell if it has medicinal uses.

No. Mandrake is known as the "root with the human shape" and was therefore supposed to be good medicine for humans. We now know that all parts of the plant are toxic.

Since exposure to summer sunlight can cause skin cancer in light-skinned elderly people, they should not garden.

Don't give up gardening! According to medical experts, light-skinned elderly people and other age groups should restrict exposure to 5 to 10 minutes around midday in June, when the sun's rays are most direct. Exposure can be longer when the angle of the sun is lower. Dark-skinned people can be exposed 5 to 10 times longer in the sun.

Sunshine produces vitamin D, which helps the body absorb calcium and hardens bones. If people cut down on milk consumption because of sodium, cholesterol, and obesity, they may face an age-related vitamin deficiency due to a decrease in milk use. Without milk and vitamin D (the sunshine vitamin), the problem of bone loss (osteoporosis) in the elderly is compounded.

We feel that gardening is a healthy activity. It makes you sweat and drink more water, and being in the sun gives you vitamin D. If you're really concerned, use protective lotion (sunblock), wear long sleeves and a hat, and work in the early and late parts of the day when the sun is lower in the sky.

Humidifiers spread a "white dust" of mildew all over the house.

The white dust is caused by minerals in your water — magnesium and calcium carbonates, and others. When the film of water sprayed by the humidifier evaporates, the minerals remain as a light coating of white mineral dust, which can aggravate respiratory problems and also damage computer disks and videotapes. You can buy cool-mist humidifiers with a built-in filter cartridge to remove the "white dust."

Latin botanical names are only important to professional growers.

We can't always use common names, like nicknames people give each other. A nickname is okay in your hometown where it has meaning to a select number — but not to everyone. A botanical name is the same the world over.

If you think Latin names are crazy now, think of how bad it was when the Greek philosopher Theophrastus classified plants according to their growth habits, floral characteristics, and life cycle. Back in those days some plants had names nine or ten words long! Can you imagine a lily with a name containing ten words?

Modern plant classification is much simpler. It was started by a Swedish botanist named Linnaeus in the mid-1700s. In his system, each plant has a two-word (binominal) Latin name (isn't that better than ten names for one plant?). The first word is the genus (the plural of genus is genera). The second word refers to the species. Example: Lilac is *Syringa* (the genus) *vulgaris* (the species). When a new plant is created and maintained under cultivated conditions, it's called a "cultivar" (shorthand for "cultivated variety"). Linnaeus's system of naming plants is one of the greatest innovations of all time!

Hybrid plants are better than nonhybrid or standard types.

Not necessarily. A hybrid is a cross between one specific variety and another genetically different variety. Such a cross can produce "hybrid vigor." The greatest value is the ability to control the offspring and their characteristics. Hybrids are more expensive because of the labor cost in creating and maintaining them. Hybrids often exhibit a wider adaptability and more uniform characteristics than do nonhybrids.

But that doesn't mean that standard or "open-pollinated" varieties are worthless. Such varieties are those that have more or less stabilized in their habits from one generation to the next. In the garden they are pollinated by wind and insects.

The topic of hybrids versus nonhybrids is too complex to cover in a single answer. Open-pollinated varieties have much to offer. Many have endured the test of time, some for several hundred years. If you have a good old-fashioned variety it could go out of existence, so one advantage of the nonhybrid varieties is that they give gardeners the option of saving their own seed. The choice is yours — you can choose either hybrids or standards or both, but it doesn't necessarily mean that hybrids are always a better bet than nonhybrids or open-pollinated types.

I've heard that companion planting doesn't work.

Plants are like people. Some plants have natural friends they like to be with, and some can't stand to be with others. This relationship is called "companion planting." The magic (or mystery) of companion planting has intrigued gardeners for centuries, but unfortunately this field has never been fully explored. Organic gardeners say there are some plants that help one another by repelling certain insects, and some plants that reject other plants. Some plants will even lessen another plant's ability to grow. Root secretions and odors all work in either repelling or attracting.

How do we feel about it? We think there's something to this study of chemical interactions between plants that inhibit or stimulate growth. There are many documented cases of allelopathy, the harmful effect of one plant on another caused by the release of chemical compounds produced by the first plant. For example, black walnuts produce juglone, which "tells" other plants to "stay away."

A recent study by Canadian researchers used marigold, nasturtium, pennyroyal, peppermint, sage, and thyme as companion plants with cabbage. The authors concluded that companion planting may improve the aesthetics of gardening, but it does little to repel lepidopterous pests (moths and butterflies) on cabbage. Our own conclusion: This study does *not* mean that companion planting is ineffective. We need more scientific tests to confirm or refute the value of companion plants. Allelochemistry (the study of chemical interactions between plants) is too new to debunk.

For Further Reading

Binetti, Marianne. *Tips for Carefree Landscapes: Over 500 Sure-Fire Ways to Beautify Your Yard and Garden.* Pownal, VT: Garden Way Publishing, 1990.

Denckla, Tanya. *The Organic Gardener's Home Reference: A Plant-by-Plant Guide to Growing Fresh, Healthy Food.* Pownal, VT: Garden Way Publishing, 1994.

The Gardener's Complete Q & A. By the Editors of Garden Way. Pownal, VT: Garden Way Publishing, 1995.

Hill, Lewis. *Pruning Simplified.* Pownal, VT: Garden Way Publishing, 1986.

Hill, Lewis and Nancy. *Bulbs: Four Seasons of Beautiful Blooms.* Pownal, VT: Storey Publishing, 1994.

Kennedy, Des. *Nature's Outcasts: A New Look at Living Things We Love to Hate.* Pownal, VT: Storey Publishing, 1993.

McClure, Susan. *The Harvest Gardener: Growing for Maximum Yield, Prime Flavor, and Garden-Fresh Storage.* Pownal, VT: Garden Way Publishing, 1992.

Osborne, Robert A. *Hardy Roses: An Organic Guide to Growing Frost- and Disease-Resistant Varieties.* Pownal, VT: Garden Way Publishing, 1991.

Powell, Eileen. *From Seed to Bloom: How to Grow over 500 Annuals, Perennials & Herbs.* Pownal, VT: Garden Way Publishing, 1995.

Riotte, Louise. *Astrological Gardening: The Ancient Wisdom of Successful Planting & Harvesting by the Stars.* Pownal, VT: Garden Way Publishing, 1989.

Riotte, Louise. *Carrots Love Tomatos: Secrets of Companion Planting for Successful Gardening.* Pownal, VT: Garden Way Publishing, 1975.

Riotte, Louise. *Sleeping with a Sunflower: A Treasury of Old-Time Gardening Lore.* Pownal, VT: Garden Way Publishing, 1987.

Sears, Elayne. *Gardening Techniques Simplified.* Pownal, VT: Garden Way Publishing, 1995.

Index

I

Insecticides and pesticides
  for blight, 124
  botanicals, 127
  diatomaceous earth, 122
  homemade versus store-bought
    sprays, 15–16, 121, 125–27
  hot pepper sprays, 124, 125
  inert substances in, 122–23
  for lawns, 84–85
  recipe for mildew and black spots,
    123
  soap solutions, 123, 125
  spraying of leaves, 15
Insects
  See also under specific name of
  effects of cold weather on, 119–20
  electric bug zappers, 117–18
  growth rate of, related to tempera-
    tures, 120
  on houseplants, 15, 16, 121, 123
  and leaf damage, 16
Irises, 33
Ivy, Swedish, 12

J

Johnson, Robert Gibbon, 60
Juglone, 47, 108

L

Lady beetles, 131–32
Lawnmowers, 80, 89
Lawns
  artificial, 82
  fairy rings in, 90–91
  fertilizers and pesticides for, 84–85
  gray, 81
  growth regulators for, 81–82
  moss in, 85–86, 87
  thatch buildup, 88–89

turfgrass, 87
  watering, 83–84
  when to seed, 87
  and wildflowers, 82–83, 92
Lead emissions, effects of, 46, 114
Leaves
  how to clean houseplant, 14–15
  as mulch, 112–13, 114
Legginess in indoor plants, 9–11
Light/light requirements, 11, 12, 13
  fluorescent and incandescent lights
    together, 13
  low light versus foot candles, 12
Light meter, use of, 11–12
Lightning, 141
Lightning bugs, 115
Lime, adding to soil, 103
Loosestrife, purple, 41

M

Maidenhair ferns, and light require-
    ments, 12
Mealy bugs, 126
Mildew, 123
Moisture meters, 97
Moles, 135–36
Moonlight, effects of, 44–46
Mosquitoes, repellents for, 116–18
Moss, in lawns, 85–86, 87
Mulch
  leaves as, 112–13, 114
  newspapers as, 108–9
  oak leaves as, 112–13
  toxicity, 110
  trees and, 112
  water loss and, 109–10
  wood wastes as, 110–11
Mushrooms
  eating wild, 53
  on lawns, 90–91
Muskmelons, ripeness in, 63–64

W

Waffle plant, and light requirements, 12
Walnuts/walnut leaves, as compost, 108
Walnut trees, planting near, 47–48
Wandering Jew, and light requirements, 12
Water/watering
  acid rain, 93
  aquarium water, use of, 94–95
  bacteria in flower vase, 34–35
  calcium and iron in, 94, 95–96
  chlorinated tap, 93–94
  collection of, on windowpanes, 13–14
  determining amount of, 7–9, 20, 97–98
  dishwater and bath water, use of, 96–97
  drainage problems, 20
  dry periods between, 9
  fluoride in, 94
  houseplants, 7, 8, 93–94, 95
  lawns, 83–84
  loss due to mulching, 109–10
  plants in the shower, 8
  and saucers, under potted plants, 7
  softeners, 95–96
  top versus bottom, 6
  trees, 73
  vegetable plants, 48
  well, 94
Watermelons, ripeness in, 63
Weather, predicting, 138–40
Weed killers, 49
Weeping fig, 10
White crust on pots/containers, 19–20
Whiteflies, 126
Wickwatering, 6
Wildflower gardens, 82–83, 92
Wood ashes, use of, 103, 114
Wood chips, use of, 111
Wood wastes, as mulch, 110–11
Woolly bear caterpillars, 138–40

Z

Zoysia, 80–81